Sky Lanterns

MĀNOA 24:1 UNIVERSITY OF HAWAI'I PRESS HONOLULU

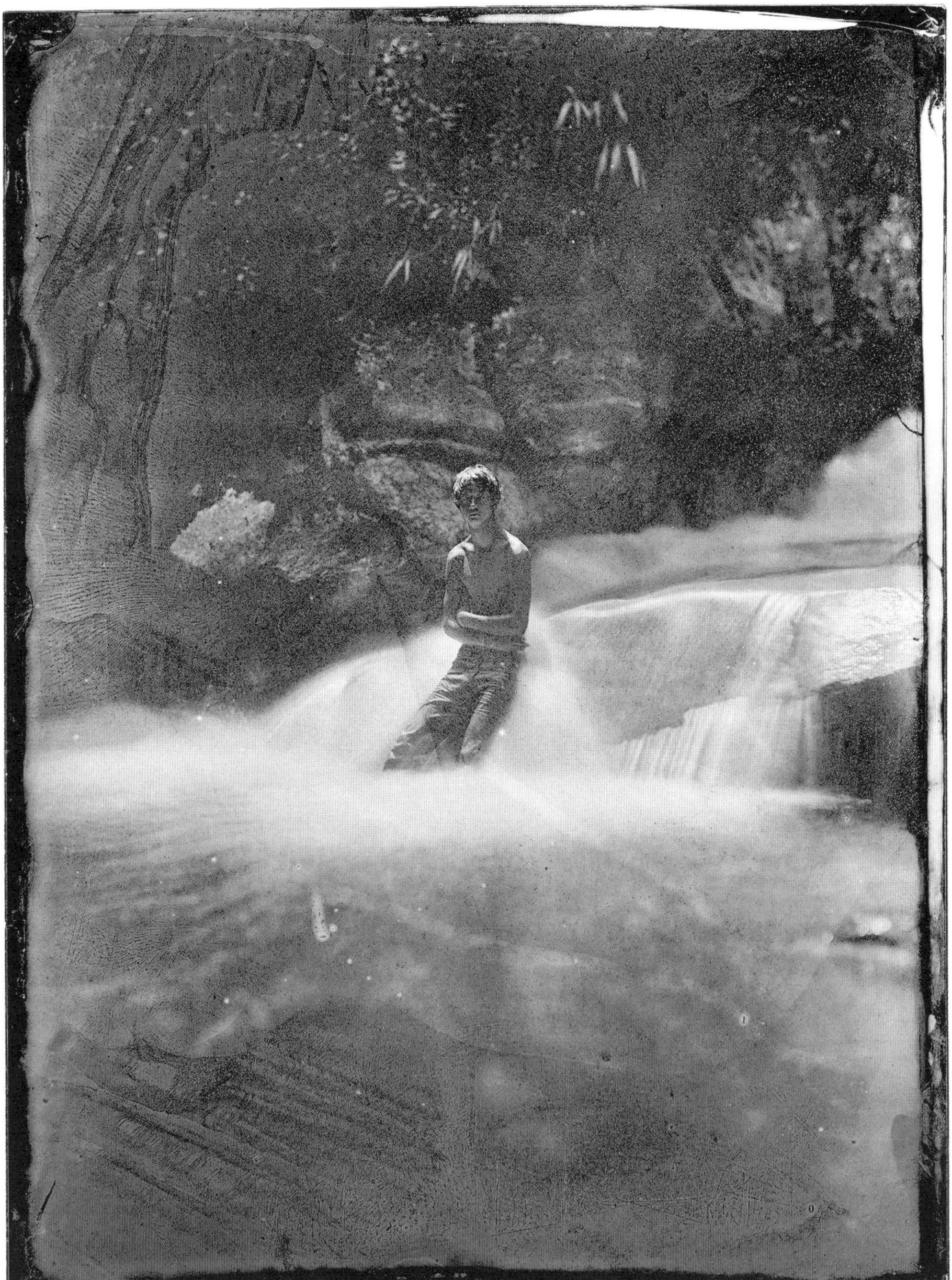

Sky Lanterns

NEW POETRY FROM CHINA, FORMOSA, AND BEYOND

Frank Stewart
EDITOR

Fiona Sze-Lorrain
GUEST EDITOR

Simple Song No. 29
Kai Fu in a stream, Zuoluodi Village
Photograph by Luo Dan
2010

Founded in 1988 by Robert Shapard and Frank Stewart

Mānoa is published twice a year. Subscriptions: U.S.A. and international—individuals $30 one year, $54 two years; institutions $50 one year, $90 two years; international airmail add $24 per year. Single copies: U.S.A. and international—individuals $20; institutions $30; international airmail add $12 per copy. Call toll free 1-888-UHPRESS. We accept checks, money orders, Visa, or MasterCard, payable to University of Hawai'i Press, 2840 Kolowalu Street, Honolulu, HI 96822, U.S.A. Claims for issues not received will be honored until 180 days past the date of publication; thereafter, the single-copy rate will be charged.

Mānoa gratefully acknowledges the support of the University of Hawai'i Administration and the University of Hawai'i College of Languages, Linguistics, and Literature; and the grant support of the National Endowment for the Arts and the Hawai'i State Foundation on Culture and the Arts. Special thanks to the Mānoa Foundation and to Daniel Tschudi.

ART WORKS.
arts.gov

HAWAI'I
STATE FOUNDATION on
CULTURE and the ARTS

http://manoajournal.hawaii.edu/
http://www.uhpress.hawaii.edu/journals/manoa/

CONTENTS

Sky Lanterns * New Poetry from China, Formosa, and Beyond

Editor's Note

While my impulse in composing this note was to think it aloud, this first sentence has already been revised more than once. Even my proposed greeting—*Dear Invisible Guest*—quirky and light as it sounded in first draft, now begs the question of spontaneity. What remains is a Czeslaw Milosz poem that floated to mind:

> The purpose of poetry is to remind us
> how difficult it is to remain just one person,
> for our house is open, there are no keys in the doors
> and invisible guests come in and out at will.
> *TRANS. CZESLAW MILOSZ AND LILLIAN VALLEE*

What kind of keys—what door—would that be? The words *keys* and *locks*—object and metaphor, adjective and qualifier—have always evoked for me an enigma: things that open as well as *enact*. The suggestive title of Bei Dao's collection *Unlock*, published in 2000, comes to mind. A new essay by him—perhaps like a key—opens this volume. As if a spiritual herald, Bei Dao makes a case in his essay for poetry as not merely aesthetic self-expression, but as work that addresses difficult social concerns, such as those arising from sweeping changes in the Chinese language. Woeser, a Tibetan exiled in Beijing, addresses these concerns by choosing to write in Chinese. Her essay moves in a borderland of fiction, reportage, memoir, and extended metaphor. Like Bei Dao, she speaks forcefully about an endangered culture and its consciousness. In their implications, both pieces unlock an inner door, and use the power and guile of understatement. Woeser's narrative style of indirection instructs and deconstructs. Bei Dao's restraint opens the way for the voices of a reply.

Knowing that Chinese poetry is represented in the international community predominantly by men's voices—an irony, given the presence of so many Chinese poets who are women—I was interested in gathering for this volume a spectrum of new women writers, from the post-Misty and post-1970s generations. Eight Chinese, Tibetan, and Taiwanese women poets—plus Asian American women poets of Chinese lineage—have contributed

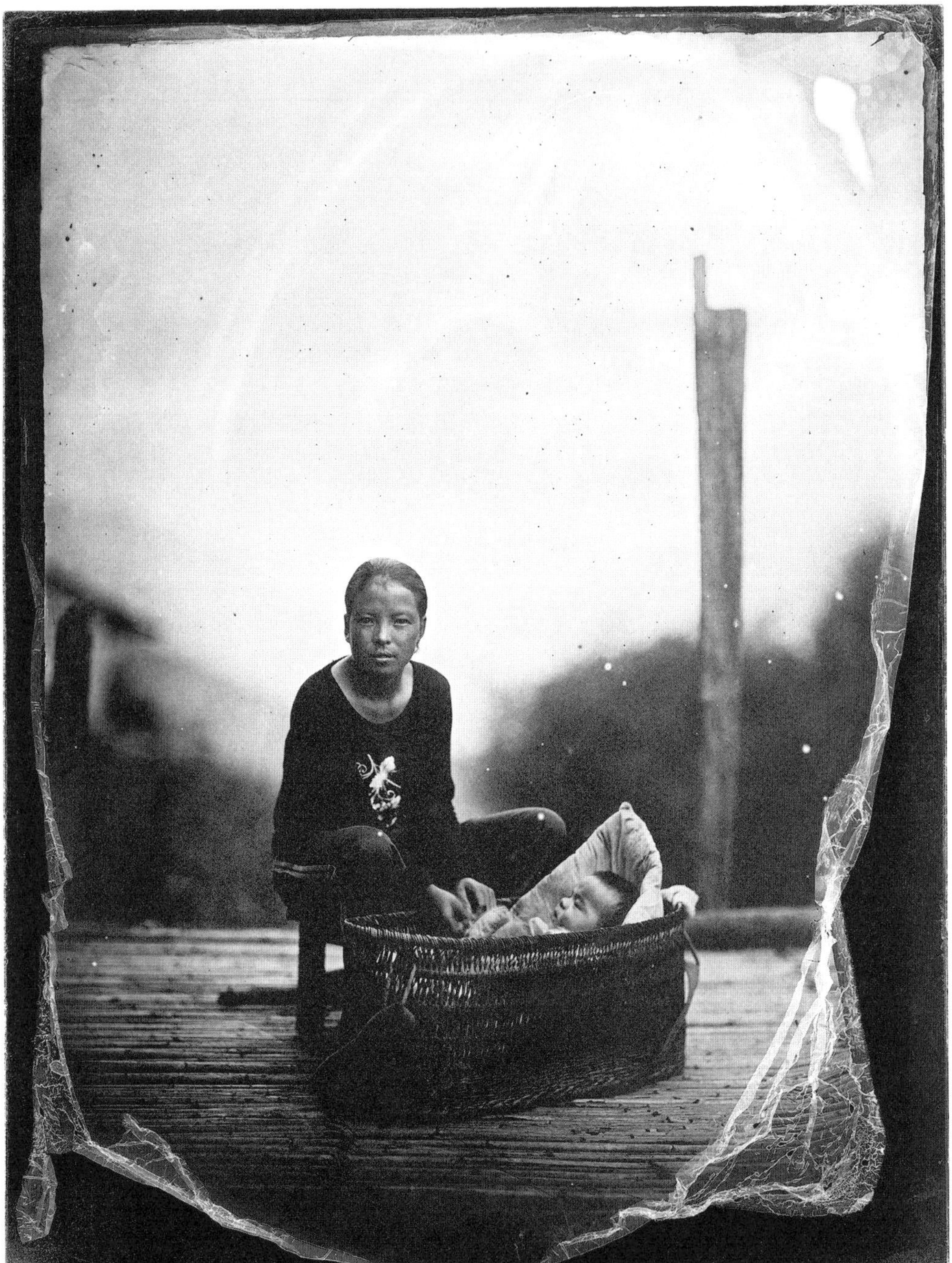

Luo Dan
Simple Song No. 5
He Yujuan and her son He Shengjie, Laomudeng Village
2010

to *Sky Lanterns*. Some are well known, others are emerging. Each offers her own linguistic surprises and poetic intelligence, and all share a preference for lyricism and epiphany.

In *A Room of One's Own*, the legendary polemic on female creativity, Virginia Woolf observes, "For it is a perennial puzzle why no woman wrote a word of that extraordinary literature when every other man, it seemed, was capable of song or sonnet." Not wanting to promote the conventional divisions by gender, however, we include contemporary male poets Wei An (1960–1999) and Hai Zi (1964–1989), both of whom died young; post-Misty generation poets Bai Hua and Zhang Zao (1962–2010); younger male poets Sun Lei and Duo Yu; and the Late-T'ang Dynasty poet Li Shangyin, a representative of the classical tradition.

For those Chinese and Taiwanese poets whose works were composed in Chinese, we have published *en face* their English translations. Most of the writings are appearing for the first time in the Anglophone world, and their translators have, with different sensibilities, sought to pursue translation as more than pedagogy and an intellectual operation. But translation—with its meaningful defeats, trials, and struggles with authenticity—is not a subject I wish to focus on here, a topic that could too quickly be substituted for the poetry itself. I like to think that the less said, the better. To each dumpling, its own filling. A dish speaks most for itself when the chef chooses to stay in the kitchen. Translation in its purest essence is neither an embellishment for cultural tourism nor a literary fashion in thrall to globalization. Li Po says it all: "This is music enough. Why tell / flutes and pipes our troubles?"

After Bei Dao's opening essay, we have presented the authors in order of age, not as a bow to hierarchy, but to trace a possibility sensitive to time. As the last on this list, I am humbled by the literary company that comes before me. As a writer, I have listened to their voices and their silences. In praise of laughter, spiritual resistance, linguistic surprises, autobiographical reticence, and creative accidents, each work greets the image and the word as a foreign friend and an intimate stranger. Over and again, each reminds us that invisible or imagined landscapes will always be lit by sky lanterns, graced by invisible guests who, like you, must have come for the full moon and a windful ride.

Fiona Sze-Lorrain
Paris, France

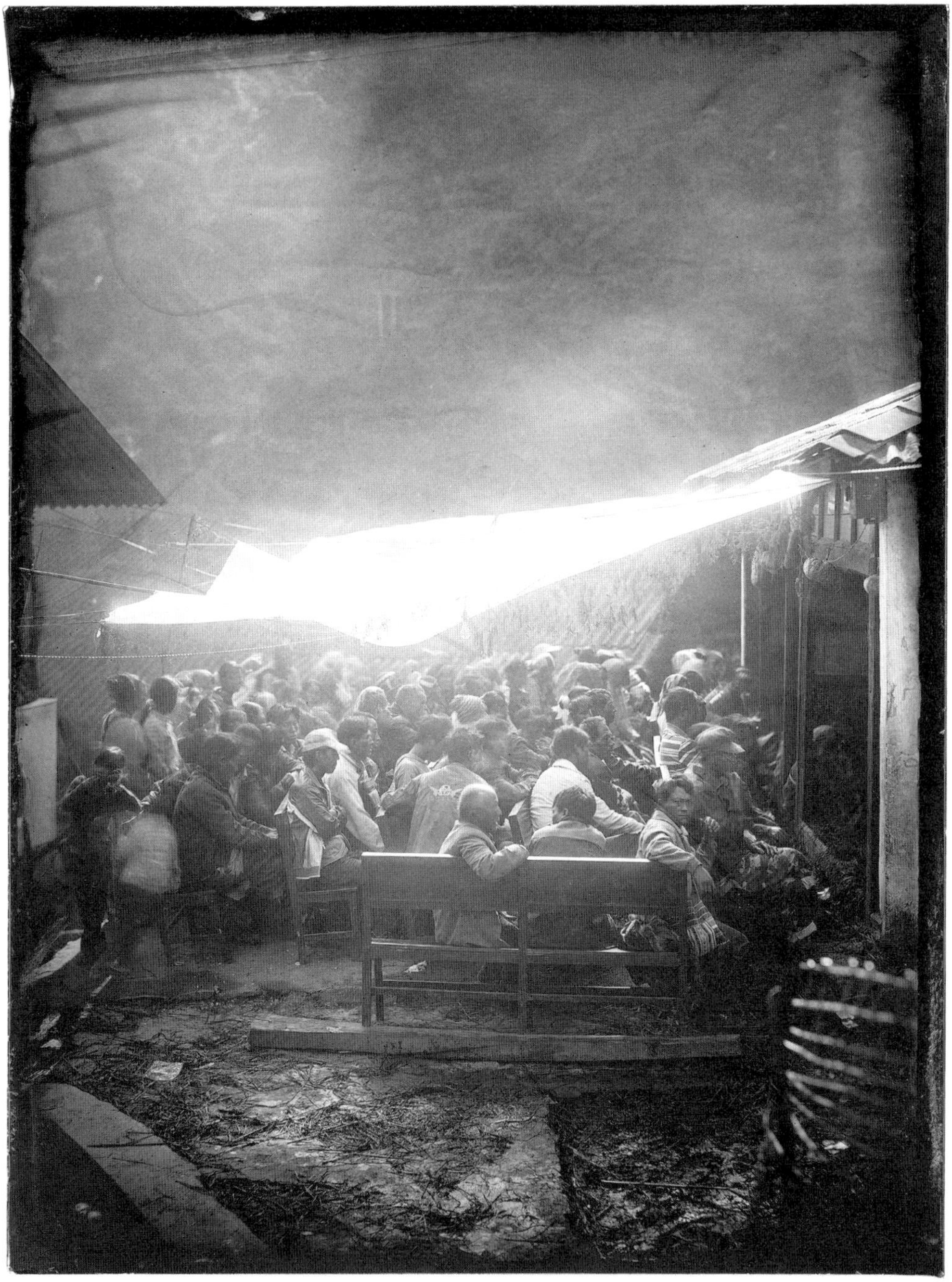

Luo Dan
Simple Song No. 1
Thanksgiving party, Wawa Village
2010

Ancient Enmity

Editors' Note

One of China's most outspoken poets, Bei Dao has lived in exile since the Tian'anmen Square demonstrations in 1989. As the chief editor of Jintian *(Today), the first non-official Chinese literary journal—founded in 1978, banned in 1980, and revived in 1990 in Sweden—he often addresses international forums about exile, censorship, and the responsibility of writers in society. In recent years, Bei Dao has been permitted to teach and reside in Hong Kong. The following essay is based on a lecture he delivered at the Hong Kong Book Fair on July 20, 2011. The translator wishes to acknowledge Sally Molini for her important editorial suggestions during the translation.*

Over a century ago, Rainer Maria Rilke wrote in his long poem "Requiem,"

> For somewhere there is an ancient enmity
> between our daily life and the great work.
> *TRANS. STEPHEN MITCHELL*

In 1900, a number of artists and writers, including Rilke, had gathered in Worpswede, a small town between Hamburg and Bremen. They attended concerts together, visited museums, and rode in horse carriages to evening festivals. Among the artists were two lovely young women, a painter and a sculptor, who were as close as sisters. Paula had blonde hair; Clara's hair was dark. Rilke preferred fair-haired Paula, but did not wish to ruin the ideal friendship he shared with them by choosing one woman over the other. After much indecision, Paula became engaged to someone else. Rilke married Clara, and she gave birth to a daughter. Seven years later, Paula died from a miscarriage and in her memory Rilke wrote "Requiem."

Perhaps knowing of such episodes help us understand better the relationship between Rilke's writing and his personal life, which can well be described as turbulent. In the four years prior to the outbreak of World War I, he lived or stayed in nearly fifty places throughout Europe. The following lines from another poem, "Autumn Day," express precisely the tension in Rilke's nomadic life:

Whoever has no house now, will never have one.
Whoever is alone will stay alone.
TRANS. STEPHEN MITCHELL

For me, the lines "For somewhere there is an ancient enmity/between our daily life and the great work" linger like the tolling of a bell—timeless and profound. In our present troubled era, they resonate particularly with those of us who are writers, compelling us to meditate on the most fundamental questions: how should we live today, how should we write, and how should we live in the world as writers true to our calling.

In Rilke's phrase "ancient enmity," the word *ancient* has a fatalistic undertone, suggesting a reference to the time of the very origins of human language. And the word *enmity,* as a metaphor, evokes a conflict that is somehow innate and paradoxical.

We might well wonder whether, if Rilke had led a stable and contented life—working as a realtor, for example, and squandering his wealth—he would have been able to write such enduring masterpieces as "Autumn Day" and the *Duino Elegies*. Likewise, we might wonder whether Kafka, if he had not lived in the oppressive shadow of his father but had instead enjoyed early success, a blissful married life, and a handsome income from the royalties of the many books he might have published—if such a Kafka could have written *The Castle* or *The Trial,* which transformed the landscape of fiction in the modern world. What if Paul Celan's parents had not died in Nazi concentration camps, and if he had not suffered the hardships of exile? Would Celan have left behind great poetry such as "Deathfugue" and "Corona"?

Who among us would not wish to have a happy life and *also* create masterpieces? Yet the "ancient enmity" in Rilke's poem is one of Fate's mysterious arrangements: that we are somehow not entitled to have both.

Of course, there may be exceptions. For instance, the American poet Wallace Stevens was the senior executive of an insurance company and had a long, tranquil life. How could he have also written such masterful poems as "The Man with the Blue Guitar," a classic of contemporary American poetry? In fact, it is possible to see, beneath Stevens's apparent tranquility, the manifestations of "ancient enmity." Ever since he was a young boy, he had always wanted to be a writer; but his father opposed him. So instead of spending his youth writing poems, Stevens studied law and, after passing the bar exam, joined an insurance company. We can imagine that in his interior life, Stevens lived with that "ancient enmity," always under the will of his father's authority.

Inspired by Rilke's verses, I would like to consider "ancient enmity" on three levels.

First, on the social level, the "ancient enmity" is the tension between a writer and his era. Regardless of the socio-political system he lives under, the writer's task is to stand apart from the mainstream, and to regard it critically as well as with distrust. Today, it is not possible for a writer to remain merely an individual craftsman, because he is also a witness to or participant in public life. This dual identity—detached from and yet part of society—is one of the strongest motivations for the writer. In other words, unless a writer is aware of the tension inherent in his dual identity, it is almost impossible to write well. Currently, the complicity of globalization with money and power has replaced the tensions that existed between East and West during the Cold War; now, all forms of orthodox ideology are a potential threat to living an authentic life. Today's globalized world is more labyrinthine and unpredictable, and thus much more dangerous than in past decades. As such, a writer in our hyper-commodified era must be wary of so-called popular speech expressions, which feed on vulgarization emerging from the realm of entertainment. Under the flag of "democratization," the art of writing is reduced to simply a tool for profiteering. A writer must guard his multifaceted perspective, responding through his work and beyond.

Further, the "ancient enmity" exists as the writer regards human society from a more expansive historical perspective. The mundane aspect of contemporary society and politics is like the passing of a cloud, merely ephemeral and superficial. To regard the breadth and complexity of human experiences beyond his time and place, a writer must have foresight.

The next level of "ancient enmity" exists in language itself. That is, the writer must recognize the strained relationship between his thoughts and the limitations of his mother tongue. Every language is perpetually changing, whether flourishing or declining. Through his work, a writer must take on the task of reinvigorating his mother tongue, especially when the language is in crisis. The Swedish poet Tomas Tranströmer referred to such a crisis when he wrote, "The language marches in step with the executioners. / Therefore we must find a new language." For over three decades, since 1949, the Chinese dwelled in the dark shadow of an "official" language known as the "Maoist style." This official language restricted the content and form of people's thoughts and speech. It even tried to subvert the forms of love. In those years, words and their associations were tightly regulated, such that, for example, "sun" was always a reference to Mao Tse-tung, "red" meant revolution, and "mother" was homeland or the Communist Party. The means by which people resisted the prison-house of the official language—language that marched "in step with the executioners"—was precisely through underground modern poetry, which was able to transform and reinvigorate contemporary Chinese speech and writing.

At present, language is in another but very different predicament, threatened by a flood of lingual rubbish. On one hand, we face the ubiquitous distortions caused by the jargons of academia, business, politics, and such areas. On the other hand, we are confronted by the massive lingual dregs and flotsam from entertainment, the Internet, and new media. At first glance, these two streams of lingual rubbish seem to be distinct, but a conspiratorial relationship exists between them. In the so-called globalized Internet era, the effect on the Chinese language is to render people as despondent and feeble as the official expressions did for three decades. Language again "marches in step with the executioners." Writers must recognize this reality, and through their work restore the freshness, plenitude, and incisiveness of language—and its power to contemplate and name the world anew.

I should pause here and explain why I say that the language of entertainment, the Internet, and new media can be as enfeebling as the Maoist language of the past. An example is the so-called fan phenomenon. Initially the concept of "fans" was limited to the realm of entertainment; in our era, however, it has spread to the literary world and to global culture. To my way of thinking, the fan phenomenon has become another manifestation of the infantilization of people by our culture. "Infantilization" is a term borrowed from depth psychology, and refers to the inclination of humans under certain pressures to voluntarily lower their level of intelligence. It is also a tendency to exploit consumer-driven globalization so as to suppress the recognition of subjectivity and suffering. As the Indian scholar Ashis Nandy has pointed out, unless there is an authentic acknowledgement of infantilization in our time, "The experience of suffering of millions will have to survive at the margins of human awareness, the way it usually does—either as fading memories handed down from generation to generation, or as fragments of an unwritten epic that cast their shadows only on the unofficial, vernacular modes of political and cultural self-expression."

Enthralled by the fan phenomenon, certain writers and scholars no longer are interested in informing the reader, but are instead constantly lowering the standard of writing in order to attract more consumers for their work, and to cater to their desires. Caught in a vicious spiral intensified by the entertainment industry, culture is ceaselessly vulgarized. In my opinion, fan phenomenon is like the "small heresies" that cults use to lure followers; the heresies seem rather harmless, but incite and bewitch, and expand out of control. The sect leader (the writer) swindles people by pandering to their sexual and other fantasies, while the disciples (fans) find psychological comfort in giving up their own will power.

The final "ancient enmity" is the tension between the writer and the self. Not only should a writer be willing to defy the world and his mother tongue, along with his cultural milieu, he should also be willing to defy himself. In my view, a serious writer must maintain heightened vigilance toward his own writing at all times.

In the preface to a recent book, I wrote, "Writing is a craft. What sets it apart from other kinds of craftsmanship is that writing is the craft of the heart. It requires an honest and sincere mind. It is a solitary craft. One must persist alone along one's path, lest writing be lost or given up at any time. In this sense, every craftsman who is devoted to writing, and accepts it as a lifelong vocation, must endure a trial of solitude in his heart. It is like walking on thin ice, held up only by one's own fear and doubt."

Hemingway wrote in *The Old Man and the Sea*, "A man is not made for defeat. A man can be destroyed but not defeated." Having witnessed the vicissitudes experienced by artists and writers of my generation, I feel deep regret and sympathy. They are a constant warning to me. Unlike those who say that many of them were defeated by money and power, I would say they were defeated by themselves. In other words, these artists and writers were no longer defying themselves, no longer competing against themselves. Truly, such self-defiance is the ultimate line of defense. If this defense falls, the writer simply surrenders completely to the world, follows its corrupt examples, and loses hope for salvation.

We live in an era beset by crises, an era that calls for continual questioning and self-examination. In such an era, writers who devote their lives to their work can find in the "ancient enmity" a concrete spiritual helm. In closing, I'd like to return to the lines from Rilke's "Requiem" with which I began:

> For somewhere there is an ancient enmity
> between our daily life and the great work.
> *TRANS. STEPHEN MITCHELL*

Frankly, what is most frightening is neither suffering nor failure, but rather ignorance and indifference. If what lies behind the billboard of a superpower is nothing but spiritual impoverishment, what is there for us to be proud of?

Translation by Fiona Sze-Lorrain

李 商 隱

三首詩

燕臺詩:秋

月浪衡天天宇濕,
涼蟾落盡疏星入。
雲屏不動掩孤嚬,
西樓一夜風箏急。
欲織相思花寄遠,
終日相思卻相怨。
但聞北門聲回環,
不見長河水清淺。
金魚鎖斷紅桂春,
古時塵滿鴛鴦茵。
堪悲小苑作長道,
玉樹未憐亡國人。
瑤琴愔愔藏楚弄,
越羅冷薄金泥重。
簾鉤鸚鵡夜驚霜,
喚起南雲繞雲夢。
雙璫丁丁聯尺素,
內記湘川相識處。
歌唇一世銜雨看,
可惜馨香手中故。

L I   S H A N G Y I N

Three Poems

SWALLOW TERRACE: AUTUMN

Moonwaves traverse the heavens, heaven's vault is sodden.
Cool Toad sets, spent. A smattering of stars descend.

Still screen of shimmering cloud, concealing a desolate face.
All night, at the western tower, the wind chimes, anxious.

A wish to weave longing into flowers, send them into distance.
Days of longing. Yet, rancor.

Only listen to the Northern Dipper, winding in orbit.
Unseen, Long River's astral waters, clear and shallow.

Red laurel spring closed with a golden fish lock.
Ancient dust fills the bed of a pair of mandarin ducks.

Worth grieving, how a little garden becomes the long road.
A jade tree is merciless to the exile.

Jasper zither quietly hiding the alleyways of Chu.
Yue gauze is cold, slight. Its gold embroidery weighted.

The parrot on the curtain hook startles at night frost,
arouses southern mists, coiling through Cloud Dream Park.

A pair of clinking pearls tied to a letter.
Recorded inside, our meeting place: Xiang River.

Witness to a lifetime of singing lips, withheld rain.
Pity, how perfume's incense ages on the hand.

霜月

初聞征雁已無蟬，
百尺樓南水接天。
青女素娥俱耐冷，
月中霜里鬭嬋娟。

房中曲

薔薇泣幽素，
翠帶花錢小。
嬌郎癡若雲，
抱日西簾曉。
枕是龍宮石，
割得秋波色。
玉簟失柔膚，
但見蒙羅碧。
憶得前年春，
未語含悲辛。
歸來已不見，
錦瑟長於人。
今日澗底松，
明日山頭蘗。
愁到天地翻，
相看不相識。

FROST, MOON

First hearing of migrating geese.
        Already, an absence of cicadas.

South of hundred foot tower,
        water touches sky.

Blue Woman, Lunar Maiden,
        both immune to the cold.

In moonlight, in frost,
        a war of radiance and grace.

CHAMBER MUSIC

Roses weep a secret pale.
An azure sash. A tiny currency of flowers.

Beauteous boy, childish as a cloud
embracing the sun, dawn, through western curtains.

The pillow is a dragon palace stone,
carved in shades of autumn waves.

Jade mattress, absence of tender skin.
All I see, silken emerald surface.

Remembering spring last year,
bitter affliction held in the mouth. No words.

Upon my return, you were already unseen.
The brocade zither outlasts the person.

Today a pine on the ravine floor,
tomorrow a cork-tree on mountain's peak.

Agony: when heaven, earth, are overturned
we will see each other, we will not be known.

Translations by Chloe Garcia Roberts

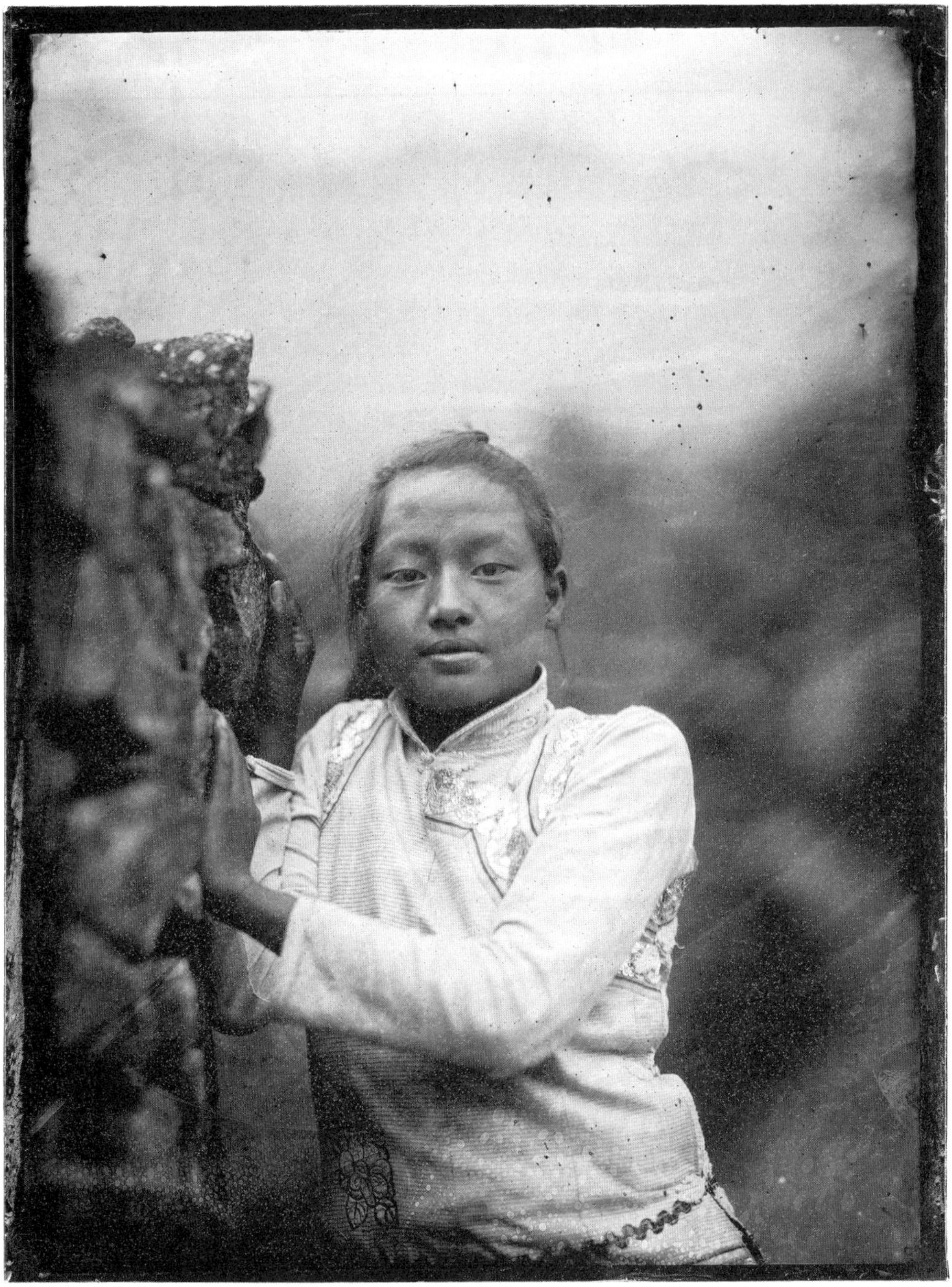

Luo Dan
Simple Song No. 2
Yu Huana from Chihengdi Village
2010

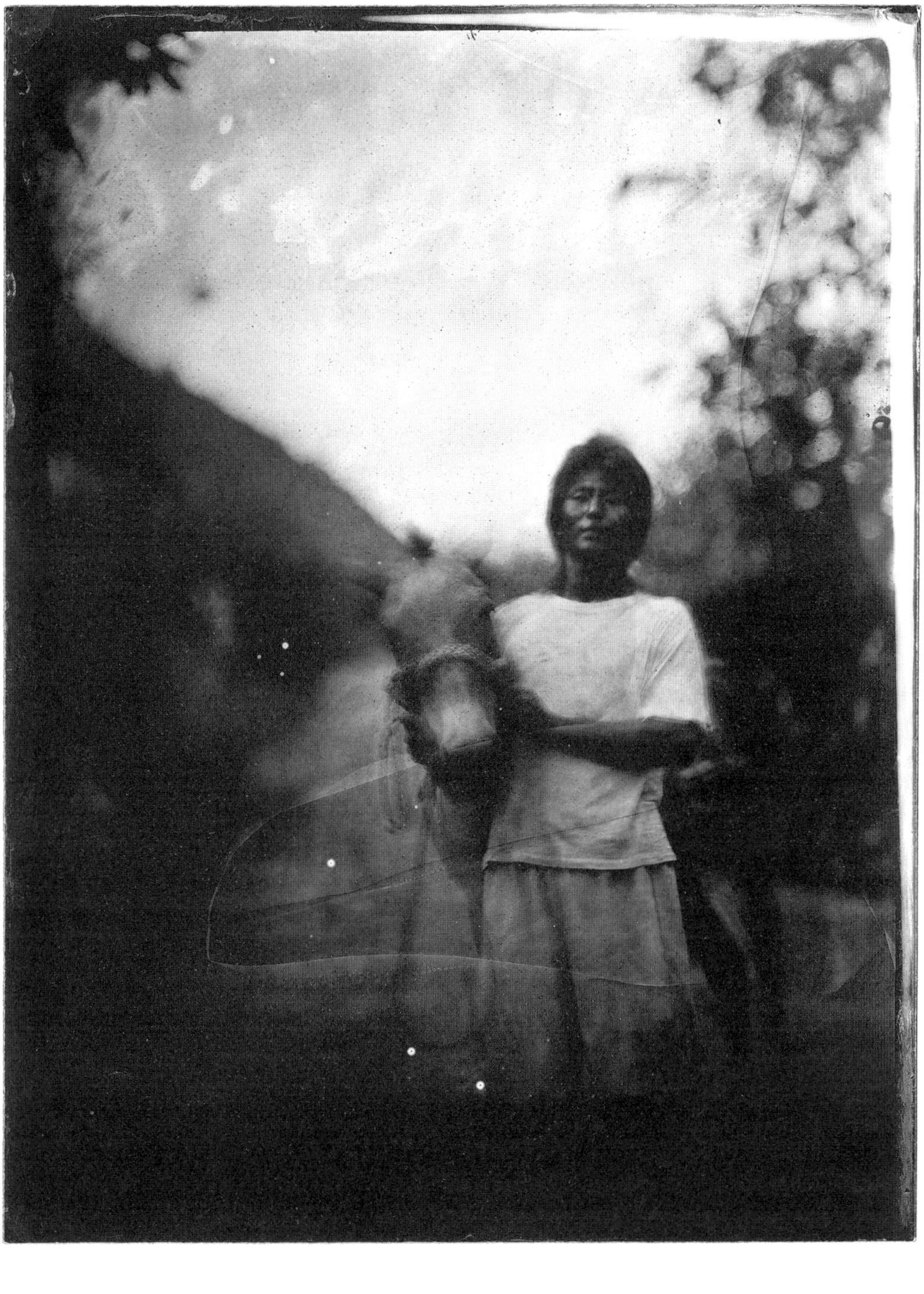

Luo Dan
Simple Song No. 9
Ai Chunhua holding his horse, Jinxiugu Village
2010

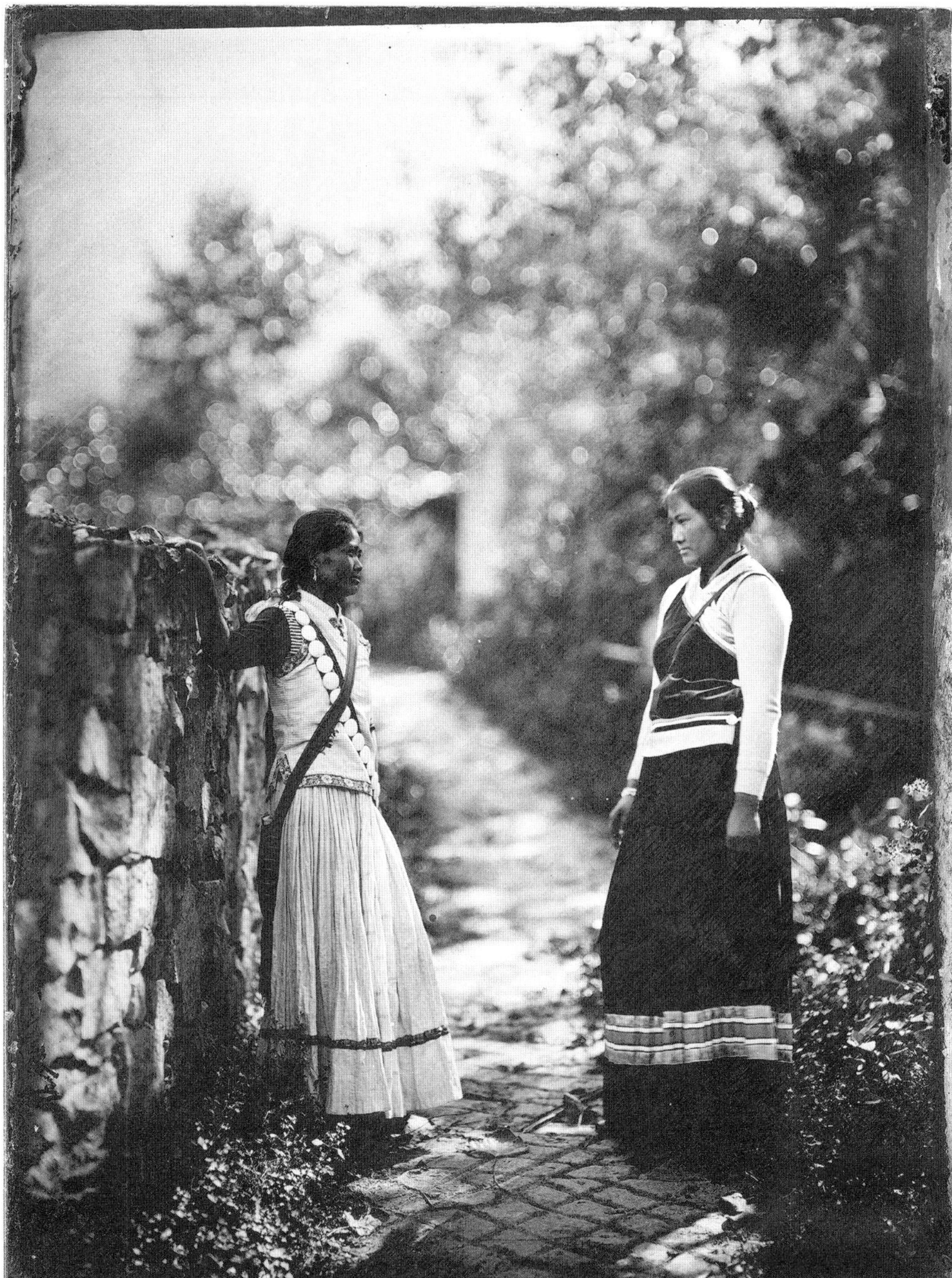

Luo Dan
Simple Song No. 24
Si Mayuan and Na Siniu, Chihengdi Village
2010

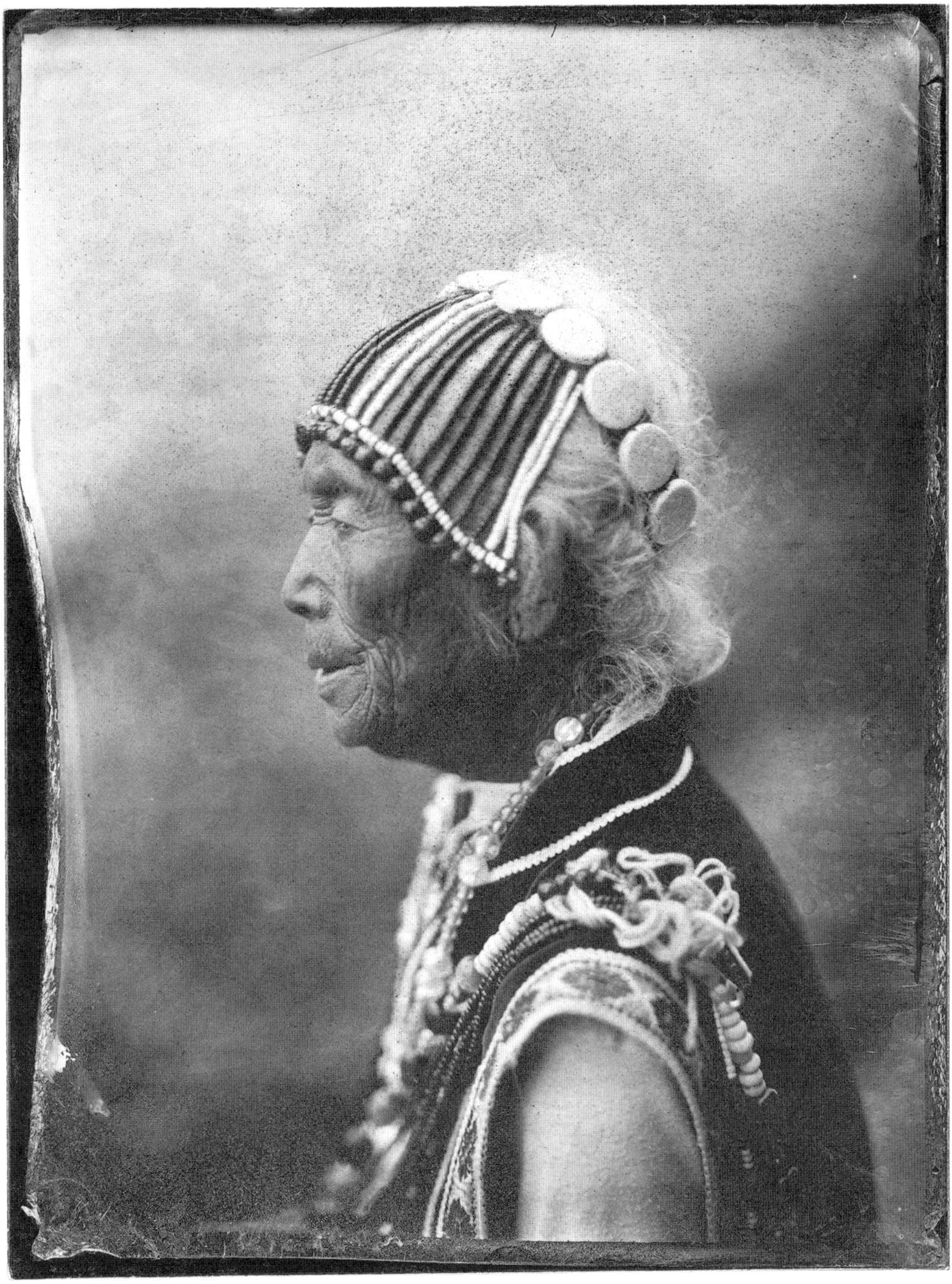

Luo Dan
Simple Song No. 7
Jin Mawei, old lady from Laomudeng Village
2010

Arctic Circle

If the strings of a 3/4 violin
are at rest, if the two horse-hair
bows repose in their case—
the case holds the blue of lakes
and the whites of snow;
she posts on a horse inside a barn;
rain splatters on the skylight
during the night; she inhales
the smell of newly born chickens
in a stall—if the interval
between lightning and thunder
is a blue dagger, if she hears
Gavotte in D Major as he drives
in silence past Camel Rock—
she stirs then drifts into feathered
waves of sleep; a healer rebuilds
her inner moon and connection
to the earth, while she plays
Hangman with her mother;
she stops running out into the cold
whirlpool dark; behind his eyelids,
green curtains of light shimmer
across the polar sky; she has difficulty
posting with one foot in the stirrup—
if he stands, at minus fifteen degrees,
a black dot in the snow—she rides
bareback to regain her balance;
he prays that diverging rays
emanate from a single quartz crystal;
he prays that her laughter be
June grass, that the jagged floating
chunks of ice ease and dissolve;

he prays when she lights a tiny
candle on a shelf; reindeer eat
lichens and browse among marshes
at the height of summer—
if she bows and hears applause
then puts her bow to the string,
if she decides, "This is nothing,"
let the spark ignite horse become
barn become valley become world.

零 雨

我和我的火車和你

1

我——有兩天沒睡好覺
內心糾葛。等一下可能會嘔吐

火車站一排大理石座椅上
我看著小書——裏面有波赫士
——或許他
和我的行李
——可以安慰我

我的淚淹到一行字上
但沒有滴下。它們不輕易
離開我。我儲存了一整座水庫
夠用好幾年

最近眼睛壞得可以壞到
可以理解波赫士了

等一下火車將經過你居住的
海洋。我將看到你。懷中有我
把我的骨頭磨出水來

我很想回家
但火車站每個人更像親人
我想站起來向他們微笑

但沒有人打擾我
我秘密地
把翅膀展開

LING YU

Myself, My Train, and You

1

I—for two days deprived of sleep
Mind tied in knots. Soon I may have to vomit

I sit on one of the station's marble benches
Reading a paperback—with Borges inside
—maybe in him
Or in my luggage
I can take comfort

Tears brim to a line of text
But do not drip. They do not lightly
Roll from me. I have stored up a whole reservoir
Enough to last me for years

My eyes are getting bad these days
Getting bad enough to understand Borges

Soon the train will pass by the ocean
Where you live. I will see you. I am in your heart
This is squeezing water out of my very bones

Wish I could go back home
But people in the station are more like kinfolk
Wish I could stand up and smile at them

But nobody bothers me
In my secret way
I unfold my wings

2

啼哭是一種自救
火車開了

淚滴到窗上
一行一行
有的不太合作
好像有些疼痛分段
進行

獨自一人時比天空
堅強。天空放聲大哭
但沒有打濕行李

行李中有何物：蠟燭
筆記本。狄董遜。我和
十九世紀。互相捏在手心

3

今天不能叫做幸福——
冷。潮濕。肚子不餓

還好。天有點昏暗。暗得
像退回到十八世紀

沒有收音機。燈泡
打更者剛留下幾道霜風

燈籠是紅色。杏花殘落
柴火點燃，下了碗細麵條——

主人書房裏的硯凍著——
粗心的奴僕被打發
到二十一世紀
借一隻快筆——

他撿到一個新名字並且
穿上主人不認識的
慢跑鞋

2

Weeping is a form of self-rescue
The train starts moving
Tears are on the window
Moving down in lines
Some will not run readily,
Like the kind of pain
That proceeds in stages

On my own I am more long-suffering
Than the sky above. The sky sobs out loud
Without wetting the suitcase

What is in the suitcase: candle,
Notebook, Dickinson. The nineteenth century
And myself, pressed in each other's palms

3

Today would be hard to describe as blessed
Cold damp air, no hunger in the gut

Could be worse. The sky looks dusky, dimmed down
As if retreating to the eighteenth century

Having no radio. No lightbulb
Chilly drafts left by the night watchman

Lantern shaded in red. Wilted almond petals falling
Kindling set alight, boil a bowlful of thin noodles—

Ink stone frozen in the master's study
Careless servant sent away
To borrow a fiber-tip pen
In the twenty-first century

He stumbled upon a new name
Tried on a pair of jogging shoes
The master would not recognize

4

火車不肯安靜
大家互相鼓動噪音

只允許一種動物
(——其他動物被禁止——)
在外面飛翔

另一頭的阮籍哭著
快和火車相遇了
(——火車喜歡走上窮途——)

大家裝瘋賣傻
說前面有一個酒窖
賣酒的娘子來自第三世紀

某些時候她觀察入微
特別重視釀酒的細節

你可以醉倒在她身旁
(——一整排火車都變成詩人——)
她會一一翻譯你身上
有酒味的詩句

5

我們在火車上讀著——
「淤泥」這個字我喜歡

我們能超越現實嗎
洗衣機的聲音
像緊箍咒

還有一種機器——能消解
矛盾嗎

我們必須在火車上
聽鋼條互相碰撞
傾軋傾軋——

宇宙太狹小了嗎
如何掘地便埋
把火車輕忽

4

The train is not in the mood to be quiet
We are all drumming up noise for each other

Only one kind of animal is allowed
(—other animals prohibited—)
To fly about outside

Over there at a dead end, Ruan Ji stands crying
Soon he will encounter a train
(—trains like to run on roads that hit dead ends—)

All of us are acting crazy
Saying there is a tavern up ahead
The barmaid comes from the third century

At times she notices subtle things
Pays heed to details of fermentation

You can lie down drunkenly beside her
(—poets line up along the whole train—)
She is able to translate each line of your body
As long as it smells of wine

5

On the train we keep reading—
"Quagmire" is a word I like

Can reality be surmounted?
The sound of a washing machine
Is like "Mantra of the Constricting Headband"

What machine do you think is capable
Of dissolving contradictions?
On the train we must listen
To steel slamming on steel bars
Pounding one against the other—

Has the universe gotten too narrow?
How does a thing get buried?
Put the train out of mind

從最初出發——這個虛無
被建構
成龐然大物

這個土木形骸
折碎之後——
(淤泥這個字——
我喜歡)

6

今天將飛躍山溝
(又過了一天)

飛躍懸崖
(又過了一天)

飛躍深淵
(又過了一天)

世紀末
是一天
世紀初
也是一天

7

我們的親密關係：無言的
互望。黑暗中
陌生的呼吸

雨打在路過的玻璃
窗上。逗點跑進來
句子貼滿牆壁

列車—著火了
正在切碎黃昏

從每個不同的站抓來詩人
故鄉是要
從何說起呢

Set out from the very beginning—this nothingness
Has been built up
Into a giant monster

Until this sturdily fashioned frame
Comes undone—
(One word I like
Is "quagmire")

6

Today we will go bounding over a ravine
(another day spent)

Leaping past a cliff
(another day spent)

Leaping over an abyss
(another day spent)

End of a century
Just another day
Start of a century
Just another day

7

Our intimacy: exchange of looks
Without words. In the darkness
Unaccustomed breathing

Rain falls on passing window
Glass. Commas splash inside,
Sentences are pasted all over the wall

Our passenger train—lit on fire
Slices the dusk apart
At every stop it grabs up poets
When the subject is one's home district
Where does one begin?

第六世紀的詩人
推敲音韻——

容貌飄搖
但是有胭脂
有油燈
還有——

誰去找回那幾隻蚊子
那頂蚊帳——

找回祖父母

8

一種存在的突顯：隱士
黑色的頭巾——

渦狀的雲杉，還是雪中的
柴扉，在燃燒——

我的心臟滾動，藏匿
在這座山中——

天翻地覆之後——葉子
落盡

伸手接住了樹枝——

幼小的獸漫行——我的
童僕，脆弱地挾一具琴

順著我的腳印，山路
蜿蜒

我的主要動脈——瀑布
傾瀉而下

(二十世紀各種主義喧嘩——)

跨過這座木橋
我的驢子嘶鳴

提醒我——正走過第四世紀的山水

A poet of the sixth century
Mulls over fine points of prosody—

The countenance wavers
But there is cochineal rouge
And an oil lamp
As well as—

Who will go and bring back a few mosquitos
That mosquito net—

Bring back my grandparents

8

Sudden evidence of existence: a hermit
Wearing a headscarf of black—

Whorled spruce boughs, or a brushwood door
In a snowscape, burning

My heart churning along, hidden
In these mountains

Once the sky stops spinning—every leaf
Floats down

Reach out to catch a branch tip

A juvenile beast goes rambling—my servant boy
Tremulously clutches a seven-string *qin*

Follows my steps along the path
Winding up and down

A waterfall—my main artery
Comes gushing down

(Noisy fracas of twentieth-century ideologies)

Crossing over this trestle bridge
My donkey brays out loud

A reminder—while I pass through a fourth-century landscape

牠將說
身體就是這麼回事

還有什麼——
能使我冰涼而
顫抖

9

炊煙。村子的心跳

我們羞於啟齒的永恆
都在其中

「野」這個字——是我的
故鄉

我想起波特萊爾。普拉斯
狄董遜。茨維塔耶娃

我添加炭火。由紅而黑
由灰而白——

我守著爐灶——
——無原因的任務

10

冬眠的時候
父親缺席

我走到另一邊
母親是火車
喉嚨低啞

咳嗽的人
站在中間——

我們經過海洋
親人一年見一次面

不得不喝酒。嗑瓜子
小孩子在某一站
開始遊戲

It brays to let me know:
This is what you can expect of a body

What else besides it
Could make me icy cold
And shivery?

9

Cooking smoke. Heartbeat of a village
To speak of eternity shames us
Yet it is found therein

The word "wilderness"—this is my
Home district

I think of Baudelaire and Plath
Dickinson and Tsvetaeva

I feed a charcoal fire. From red to black
From gray to white—

I watch over a stove
—Task without a reason

10

In a time of hibernation
Father's seat is empty

I turn to the other side
To the train that is Mother
Her voice is low and grating

The person who coughs
Stands between us—

We ride past the ocean
Kinfolk see each other once a year

We can't help but drink liquor, crack melon seeds
Once we pass a certain stop
Children begin playing

我們非常需要小孩
祭祀。寫日記

我的喉嚨非常癢
所有的注意力集中——

把眼淚擠出
丟進海洋——

身體內部——

We need children terribly
To make offerings. Keep diaries

Our throats are terribly scratchy
All attention on a single point—

Squeeze out some tears
Throw them into the ocean—

Within the body—

Translation by Denis Mair

陳 育 虹

五首詩

蟬嘶

另一種六月雨
倏忽傾盆而至倏忽
停歇，靜止

另一種蔭影
厚，密，鋪天蓋地
卻說不清形跡

另一種酒
飽和，持重，藏不住
亟待奔流的激情

另一種頻率
穿越第四維度
傳給某個透明的耳朵

另一種詩
寫在六月潮溽的心
又倏忽蒸發

關於二月十四的天氣……

我寫下關於霧像一隻貓
關於風的分身術
西北風七級我們必須安撫的記憶
關於雨的飛蛾流竄
因為貼近了冷氣團

海洋思考著星座與潮位
浪向四十五度週期六點二秒
浪高三呎救生艇從甲板滑落

CHEN YUHONG

Five Poems

CICADA SONG

another June rain
swiftly pours swiftly
rests, to a halt

another shadow
thick, dense, omnipresent
yet traces, inexplicable

another wine
saturated, prudent, unveiled
demands torrents of passion

another frequency
through the fourth dimension
transmitting to a transparent ear

another poetry
written in June's humid heart
and swiftly evaporates

CONCERNING THE WEATHER, FEBRUARY 24...

I write about fog like a cat
about wind's ubiquity
northwest wind at force 7 a memory we must appease
about moths of rain fleeing in all directions
nestled against masses of cold air

sea meditates on stars and tidemarks
waves at 45 degrees last 6 minutes 2 seconds
waves 3 feet high lifeboat slides off deck

未及交代什麼
乾潮滿潮乾潮滿潮潮浪踮著腳

在懸盪的繩索奔跑
一尾抹香鯨潛回海底
潛入我們一疋薄光的午後
此刻累積雨量九十毫米
潮浪席捲的沙灘有蒼鷺來回尋找

過中天的紫繡球
雲還在永凍層我寫下
關於霧的嚅囁夢囈經唪聲在耳邊
關於海的狂草
不停寫著又嘩嘩撕掉

白色蝴蝶蘭

你聽見它墜下
乾澀的摩挲聲更像
一張紙，搓皺了扔棄
你拾起來，閱讀
紙面字跡已不可辨識

美麗已不可辨識
豐腴的花瓣沒有染著
嫩黃的心甚至不曾一隻蝶
吻
它也感覺些微失落嗎

而怎麼一生就過了
在離莖的剎那
細弱的摩挲聲更像一字
偈，乾淨的
寫在夕陽的窗前

yet to explain anything
low tide high tide low tide high tide tides tiptoe

run with a dangling rope
a sperm whale dives deep into sea
into our afternoon a slice of thin light
at this time rain accumulates at 90 mm
on shores swept by tides herons return to seek

purple hydrangea over midday
clouds are still a permafrost I write
concerning stammer somniloquy chants of fog by the ear
concerning wild cursive calligraphy of sea
writing and tearing non-stop

Translations by Fiona Sze-Lorrain

WHITE MOTH ORCHID

you hear its falling
the dry scraping sound like
a piece of paper, crinkled and discarded
you pick it up to read
traces of words, now barely legible

beauty beyond recognition
hardly any colors in its opulent petals
its pale yellow heart never kissed
by a butterfly
did it too feel this as a loss?

and a lifetime has passed
at the instant of parting from the stem
the minute scraping sound like
a one-word Buddhist riddle to provoke
enlightenment before the twilight window

(2011)

失眠

平攤者
一塊疲軟的薑餅

清早還留著夜的
牙印兒

最初

願意回到一株裸蕨
一滴雨的原點

那時火山與冰川還沒有成形
翼龍成群飛越換日線
抹香鯨與麒麟在草地嬉戲

回到一雙眼不含砂礫
一雙手未曾結繭

看，觸撫且嗅聞
夜的糅雜如獨行的貓
舔舐墨綠的風是薄荷在齒間

再一次，願意
回到最初那一雙耳

像河蚌
薄得透明
過濾你藻草般的呼吸

INSOMNIA

lying flat
a limp piece of gingerbread

when dawn comes, the night's teeth
marks are still visible on it

(2011)

Translation by Michelle Yeh

AT THE BEGINNING

willing to return to the beginning
of an extinct fern, or a raindrop

long before volcanoes, before glaciers
winged dragons that fly in flocks across the date line
musk whales and Qilins that frolic on grasslands

return to a pair of eyes without the grit of sand
a pair of hands without calluses
look, touch, and smell
the hybrid night like a cat hunting alone
tasting the forest-green wind of chewed mint

willing to once again
return to the very beginning, a pair of ears

like river clamshells
so thin and translucent
they filtrate your algae breath

(2011)

Translation by Michelle Yeh and Frank Stewart

杨 炼

女婴

——致被溺死的女婴

你小得不值得那阵冷　水呛进
袖珍版的肺　袖珍的爆炸鲜而嫩
你小得不值得一种碎　只一瞬
血丝洇开红花　缕缕迎着母亲

被溅湿的手　仍是世界上
最美丽的手　水滴刻着牙印的咬伤
浸没一半时　你的雪堆在塌方
死死按在水底　小得不抽动的汪洋

直接连着子宫　你的眼睛
没睁开才看清末日　你的命
是一串否认的水泡　凸出哭叫的性
一道印在你所有器官上的禁令

你必须死　为了可能生的弟弟
立刻死　水快于爱　掐紧这周期
小小的浑浊被更小的四肢搅起
又静了　母亲溶解成剧毒的名字

Baby Girl

to a deliberately drowned baby girl

you're so small you're not worth that chill   water choking
pocket-sized lungs   pocket-sized explosions fresh and tender
you're so small you're not worth breaking   in an eyeblink
bloody streaks diffuse into red flowers   each one welcoming mother

splashed hands   still the loveliest
hands in the world   each droplet a toothmark
when you're half-sunk   your snowdrift collapses
pressed under water   a sea so small it doesn't shudder

tied to the womb   your eyes
closed to witness your final moment   your fate
is a chain of bubbles of denial   the wailing bulge of your sex
all of your organs stamped prohibited

you have to die   for the possibility of a younger brother
die right away   water quicker than love   nip off this cycle
small eddy stirred by smaller limbs
and silenced   mother dissolves into a toxic epithet

Translation by Brian Holton

柏 桦

四首诗

下午

焦虑的寂静已经感到
在一本打开的散文里
在一首余音缭绕的歌里
是的，我注意到了
还有更重要的一点
某个人走进又走出

入睡前你一直在沉思
徒劳的镜子凝视着什么
即将切开的水果
或棕色的浅梦

下午你睡得很稳
脾气也成了酒
是的，我注意到了这一切
包括窗帘有一点美丽
你的梦在过渡

这是最好的时间
但要小心
因为危险是不说话的
它像一件事情
像某个人的影子很轻柔
它走进又走出

1985 春

BAI HUA

Four Poems

AFTERNOON

you can feel an anguished stillness
in an open book of prose
in a song that spirals
yes, I notice
something more fatal
a man is walking in and out

before sleep you contemplate
a vain mirror stares
fruits to be sliced
or a brown light dream

you sleep well in the afternoon
even your temper has become wine
yes, I notice all these
even the faint beauty of curtains
your dreams are in transition

this is the best moment
but take care
for danger is silent
like an incident
a shadow, light and soft
it walks in and out

(Spring 1985)

献给曼杰斯塔姆

那个生活在神经里的人
害怕什么呢？
害怕赤身裸体的纯洁？
不！害怕声音
那甩掉了思想的声音

我梦想中的诗人
穿过太重的北方
穿过瘦弱的幻觉的童年
你难免来到人间

今天，我承担你怪僻的一天
今天，我承担你天真的一天
今天，我突出你的悲剧

沉默在指明
诗篇在心跳，在怜惜
无辜的舌头染上语言
这也是我记忆中的某一天

牛已经停止耕耘
镰刀已放弃亡命
风正屏住呼吸
啊，寒冷，你在加紧运送冬天

焦急的莫斯科
你握紧了动人的肺腑
迎着漫天雪花，翘首以待
啊，你看，他来了
我们诗人中最可泣的亡魂！
他正朝我走来

我开始属于这儿
我开始钻进你的形体
我开始代替你残酷的天堂
我，一个外来的长不大的孩子
对于这一切
路边的群众只能更孤单

1987年11月

TO OSIP MANDELSTAM

What does the man who lives in folly
fear?
The purity of a naked body?
No! Voices—
voices free of thoughts

My dream poet
travels through the heavy north
the weak illusory childhood
You can't help but arrive in this world

Today I'll bear your eccentricity
shoulder your innocence
heighten your tragedy

Silence points out—
The heart of poetry is beating, lamenting
An innocent tongue is dyed with language
This is also a memorable day

Cows have stopped plowing
Sickles have quit toiling
Wind holds its breath
O cold, you hasten to drive winter away

Anxious Moscow
you tighten your poignant organs
waiting before the snowy sky
Ah, look, he is here
The most tragic ghost among us poets!
He is walking toward me

I begin to belong here
to enter your body
to replace your cruel heaven
I—a foreign child who never grows up
In face of these
roadside masses feel only lonelier

(November 1987)

初春

啊，来了，哈哈大笑的春天来了
那牢底已坐穿

再过三天就放学
那翅膀硬了的鸟可以飞了

孩子们在打着包裹
孩子们用手勾画长征的道路

而其中一个孩子举着羊头痛哭
他吵着要穿一件夏天的衣服

1991年2月

吐蕃男子

吐蕃男子持铁，下颌长出毛就用钳子拔去。
吐蕃男子不弃，用死去父母的头颅做成钵和杯子。
而巫师吃人肉，召唤好天气；
而祭师切尸体，引来天空的神鹰。

某个吐蕃男子有狭长的仪表——
一月弯刀；
某个吐蕃男子风马凌空
不重
恍如掠过水面的燕子……

2010年12月3日

SPRING BEGINS

Ah, here it is, the laughing spring is here
Prison is over

School ends in three days
The bird with hardened wings can now fly

Children are packing up
tracing the Long March with their hands

A child holds up a goat head and wails
He is crying for summer clothes

(February 1991)

THE TIBETAN

the Tibetan is holding iron, when his underjaw grows hair
  he pulls it out with pliers
the Tibetan does not give up, uses his parents' skulls for earthen
  bowls and cups
the sorcerer eats human flesh, summons good weather
the priest cuts a corpse, lures condors from the sky

a certain Tibetan has a long, narrow look—
a moon a sickle
a certain Tibetan soars like a wind horse
light
like a swallow skimming over water

(December 3, 2010)

Translations by Fiona Sze-Lorrain

伊 路

六首诗

两个瓷瓶

第一天 我看见它——
春风 春水 荷花 荷叶 莲蓬
摇摆 迷人 纷乱……
瓶口至底有一尺多深的暗和静
我把手伸进去
像伸进一个凉凉的潭
我抱住它
一直抱到旅馆的房间里

第二天 它在等我——
野山 野树 野溪 野云 石桥 瓦屋
一排淡淡的鸟不知要飞去哪里……
我也去抱住它
像抱着一个故乡
一腔的空
很轻

我把它们抱到回程的火车上 抱到我家客厅
有时它们会一高一低地浮动进烟尘 那年
上海的街头
有很多孤独的瓷瓶

一棵老的树

银色的树干 疏朗地张开
没有很细的枝 没有叶子
风暴走得干干静静

被丛林的茂密和阴暗
衬得

YI LU

Six Poems

TWO PORCELAIN VASES

The first day   I see it—
spring wind   spring water   lotus   lotus leaf   lotus seed
swaying   alluring   swirling . . .
several inches of dark and quiet at the bottom of the vase
I reach my hand inside
like reaching into a cool deep pond
I hold it in my arms
holding it all the way to my hotel room

The next day   it waits for me—
wild mountain   wild tree   wild creek   wild cloud   stone bridge
    tiled house
who knows where a misty row of birds might fly
I also hold it tight
like holding a homeland
a chestful of space
very light

I hold them in my arms to my returning train   to my living room
sometimes they float high and low into dust   this year
in the streets of Shanghai
there are many lonely porcelain vases

AN OLD TREE

Silver bark   opens cheerfully
without fine branches   without leaves
the storm has left cleanly and quietly

contrasted by
the dense and bleak forest

如白白的水流
仿佛它植根的山
是一座湖

像不谙世事的老奶奶
连眼泪都是淡的
手指也很凉

回望 只有它
如玉雕
养在天穹的身体里

只有它
像一个烂漫的玩具
吊挂着星斗和天籁
摇起来会叮叮咚咚响
想飞就飞起来

早春

忽然发现整片原野唯一在动的是
　　四只牛的尾巴
庄重如凝着风暴
一撩一拨都似叮咛
牛低沉的头仿佛和身后的尾巴无关
牛也仿佛与自己无关
被它啃进的青草是否也和肠胃无关
四条拂天拍地的尾巴间
多了一只翻山越谷的蝴蝶
这蝴蝶也仿佛与它自己无关

一挂飘忽的楼梯

别人以为你睡了
可你脑子里的河山正在展开
高山 大海都能调遣来
天庭湛蓝完整 白云飘
繁忙的街道从中穿过
一个模糊的聚会 在年代的远景里

后来你真的睡着了
就仿佛进入天堂或地狱

like white water
as if its mountain taking root
is a lake

like an unsophisticated old grandmother
even tears are so plain
fingers are also cold

looking back   only it
like jade sculpture
grows inside the heaven's vault

Only it
like a carefree toy
droops with stars and sounds of nature
rings like a ding-dong bell when it shakes
flies when it wants to fly away

EARLY SPRING

suddenly I found the only stirring in the fields
        the tails of four cows
as solemn as a congealed storm
each swish an urge
their bowed heads seem unrelated to their tails
each cow also seems unrelated to itself
is the grass it eats also unrelated to its stomach
between their four tails
over canyons and hills comes a butterfly
even the butterfly seems unrelated to itself

A FLIGHT OF FLOATING STAIRS

others think you're asleep
as landscapes unfold in your mind
high mountains   oceans can be lured here
a full and azure sky   white clouds float
a bustling street weaves through
a hazy reunion   in the distance of time

later you really fall asleep
like entering heaven or hell

这里走走 那里瞧瞧 推门进去
已故的亲人都神采奕奕

猛然睁开眼睛
又是一个世界 很亮 有声有色
似乎还有一个地下室
自动封闭起来

如果把一个人简化再简化
就是一挂飘忽的楼梯
在尘世的各处碰来撞去

有没有这样的一只鹰

一

有没有一只鹰在寻找一片花地
看见一只蝴蝶 生起羡慕之心
有没有一只鹰想蹲下来
同情一只在草棚里下蛋的母鸡
有没有一只鹰敢蔑视仰望
不要趁着下雨的时候流泪

有没有一只鹰肯承认 那樱桃大的心脏里
并没有闪电 风暴和冰雹
只有一腔温热的血

二

有没有一只 会心酸的鹰
为生病的小鹰忧愁的鹰 神经衰弱的鹰
说很累的鹰
为什么人们都把鹰说成雄鹰呢

看见云朵了吗
它是多么柔软
无底无边的天空
也像爱 像悲伤
没有方向和结果

畅通不是更密的栅栏吗
没有阻挡不是更不饶人的围困吗
有没有一只鹰因此而谨慎 不安

wandering here   looking there   pushing open a door
all your dead kin are glowing with health

eyes suddenly open
yet another world   very bright   very vivid
there is also a basement
sealing up by itself

if you simplify a man again and again
he'll just become a flight of floating stairs
knocking here and there in this world of dust

IS THERE SUCH AN EAGLE

1

Is there an eagle who seeks a flowerbed
sees a butterfly   grows envious
Is there an eagle who wants to squat down
pities a hen laying eggs in a straw shed
Is there an eagle who dares to scorn the sky
does not cry when it rains

Is there an eagle who admits   in its cherry-sized heart
there is no lightning   no storm no hail
just an urge of warm blood

2

Is there an eagle   who knows a bitter heart
worries for its sick baby   suffers from depression
says *I'm so tired*
Why do people always think an eagle is a male

Do you see the cloud
It is so tender
The limitless sky
is like love   like sorrow
without direction or consequence

Isn't *clarity* a more refined barrier
Isn't *obstacle free* a more merciless blockade
Is there an eagle who will feel guarded   and ill at ease

三

有没有一只鹰肯让意志弯一弯
像被风吹动 让春燕过去的柳丝
或像攀缘大树的藤萝
如果真有这样的大树呢

有没有一只鹰把眼睛放在天外
看见自己渺小的翅膀
说怕 恐惧

有没有一只鹰羽毛纷乱
躺在山冈 对一株小草说：
已竭尽全力
但无法飞完天空

想起你的出生

当我的身体
棉纸般薄在产床上
护士正把你昂起的粘着血点的四肢
摁到盛着水的盆里

是此刻黄昏虚弱的红日
使我想起你的出生

看见一个更大的盛水的盆
等着接纳它

3

Is there an eagle willing to bend its will
like a willow moved by wind   making way for spring swallows
or like a wisteria winding up a tree
if there is such a tree

Is there an eagle who sees from beyond the sky
sees its own tiny wings
says *I'm scared   I'm terrified*

Is there an eagle whose feathers flutter
lies on a hill   tells the grass
All my strength is exhausted
I can't fly the whole sky

RECALLING YOUR BIRTH

when my body
lay thin on a delivery bed, like cotton paper
the nurse pressed your dangling bloodstained limbs
into a basin of water

this dusky, frail red sun
recalls your birth to me

as I see a larger basin of water
waiting to receive it

Translations by Fiona Sze-Lorrain

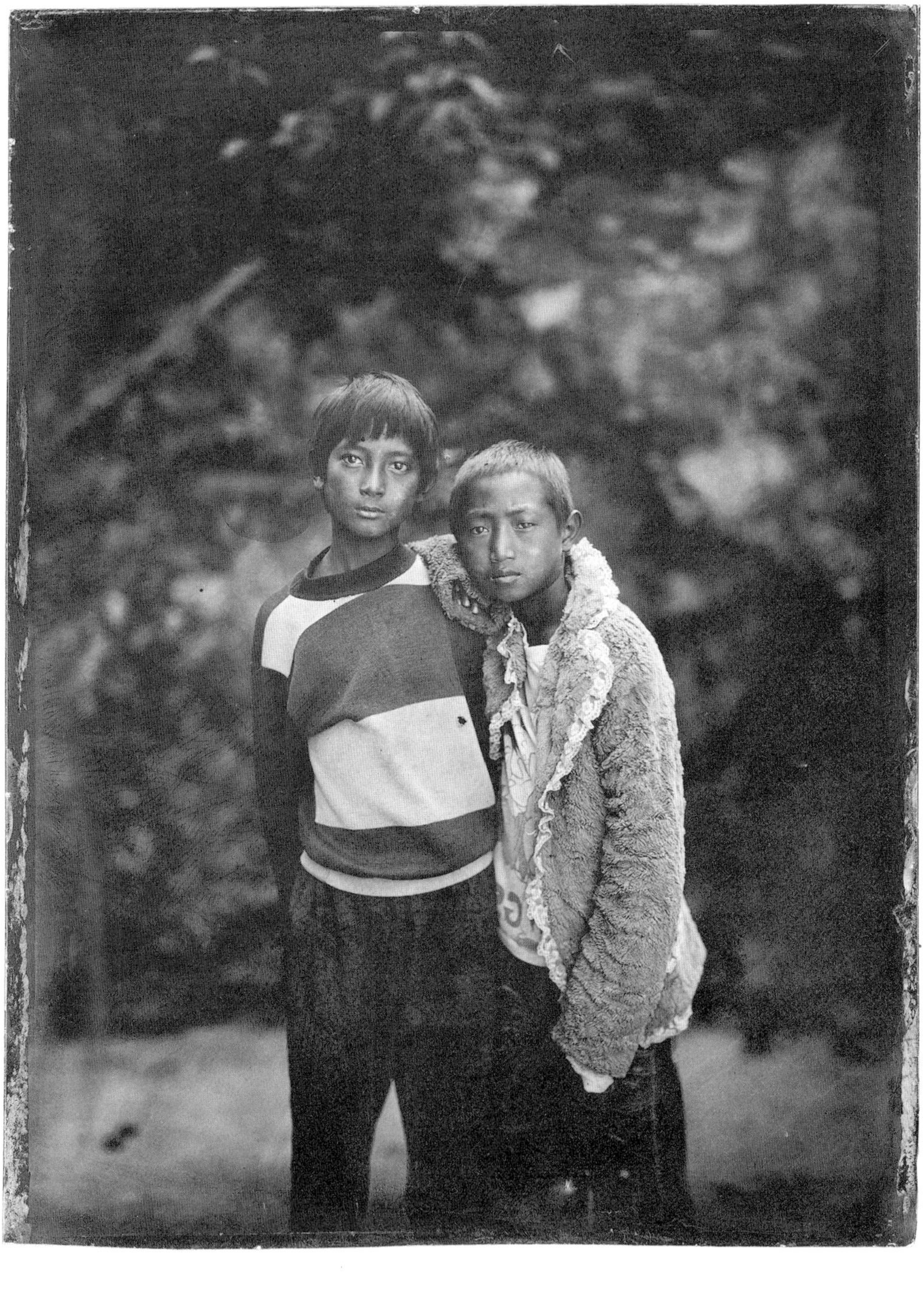

Luo Dan
Simple Song No. 16
The boys, Ken Shahua and Deng Nusheng, Mugujia Village
2010

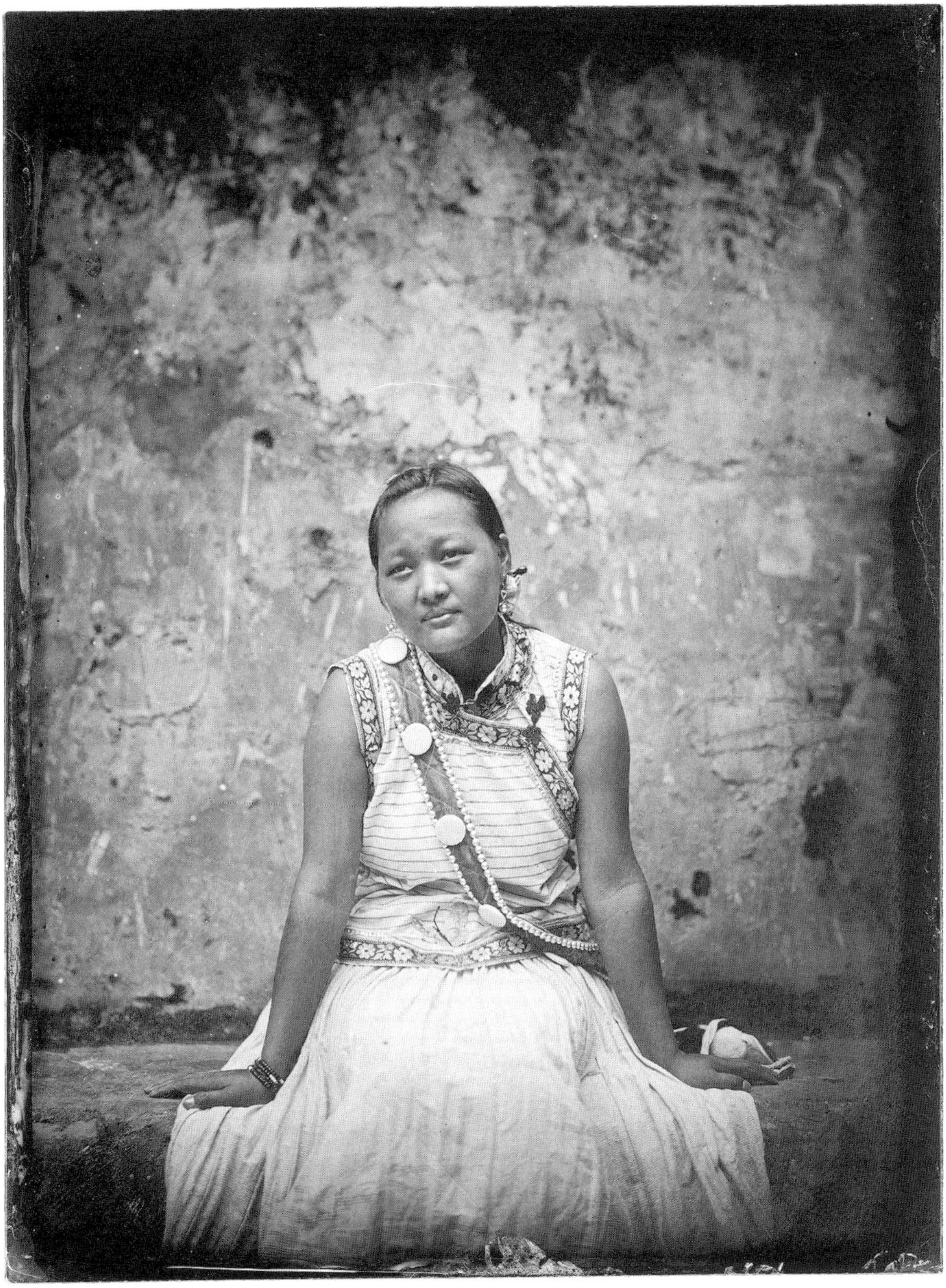

Luo Dan
Simple Song No. 6
Yu Yufen, Aludi Village
2010

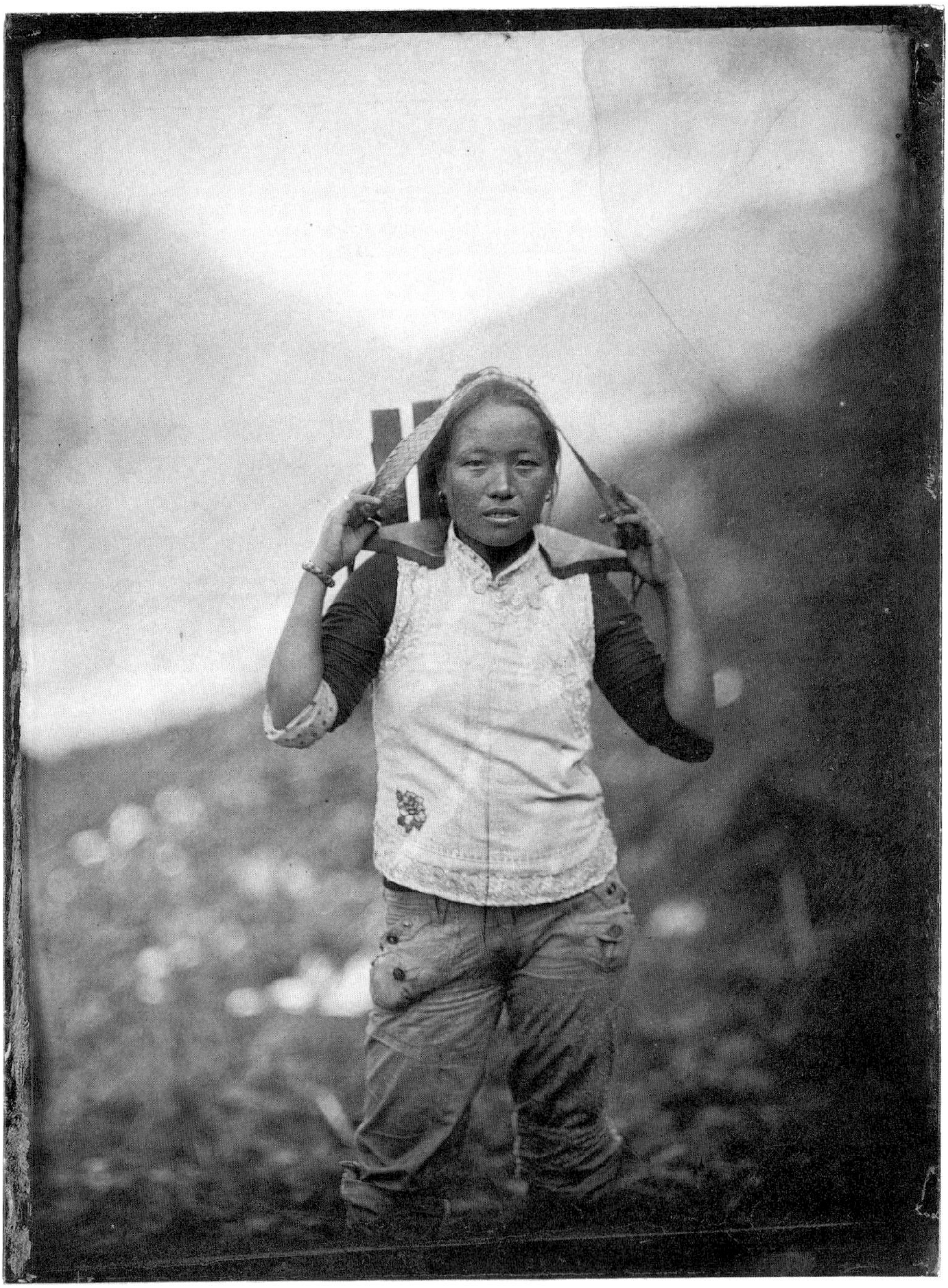

Luo Dan
Simple Song No. 13
A girl carrying stones, Buladi Village
2010

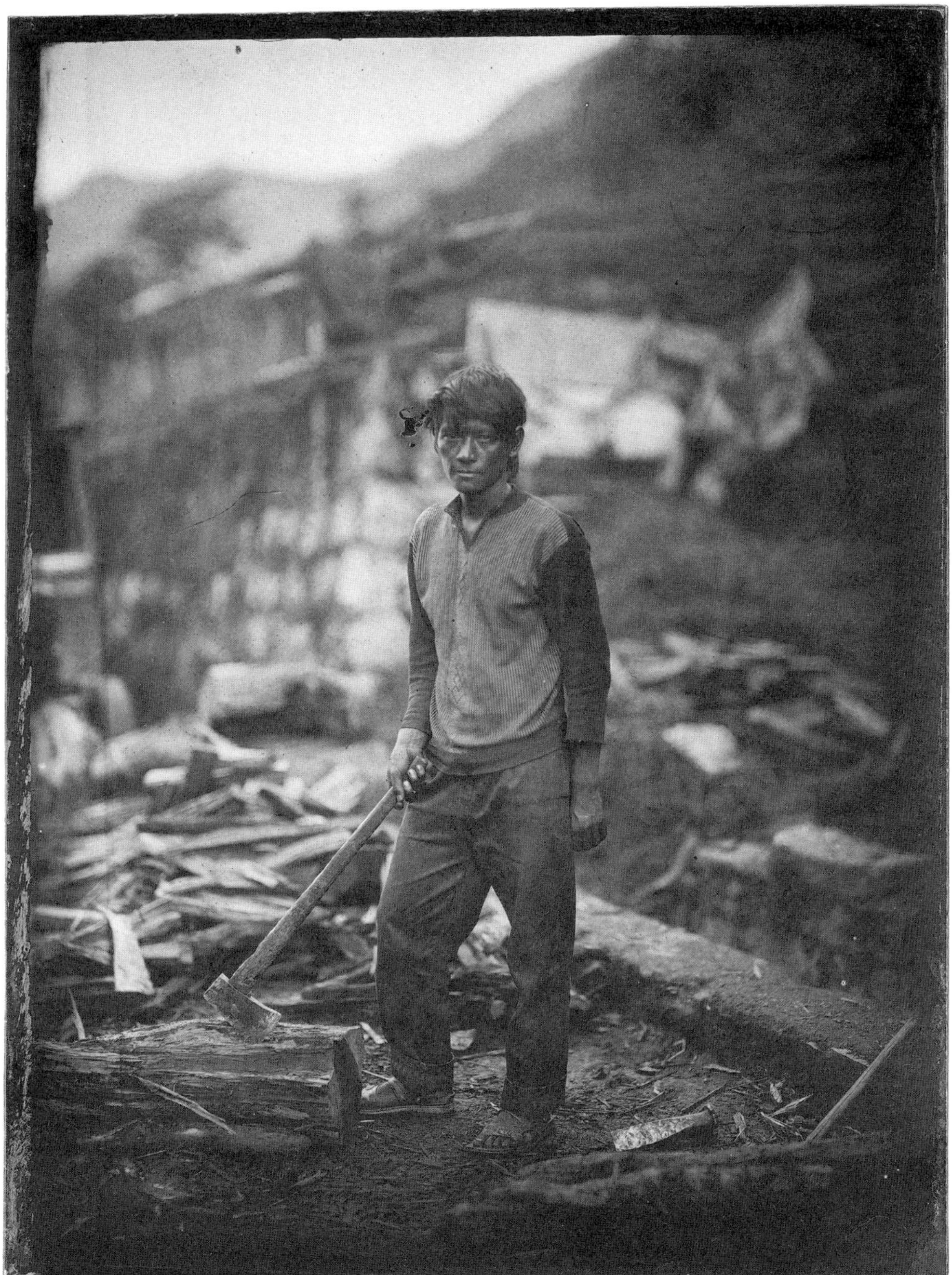

Luo Dan
Simple Song No. 20
Yi Sihua splitting firewood, Buladi Village
2010

WEI AN

from *Life on Earth*

Translator's Note

Recently, Wei An's sister and brother took me to see his apartment, in the Beijing suburb of Changping. With us were three of Wei An's friends: his college classmate Zhou Xinjing, the poet Shu Cai, and the novelist Ning Ken. Wei An's basketball, camera, and canvas traveling bag are still hanging inside the front door, and his study is just as he left it when he died in 1999. On the bookshelves are Chinese translations of the foreign writers he admired, and in a box on a bottom shelf are his manuscripts. Between 1988 and 1995, he wrote seventy-five brief meditations on the things that he observed and cared about.

Wei An wrote sparingly, and he wrote slowly. His meticulous self-editing was one of the qualities that puzzled and charmed his friends. Those with me that day reminisced, agreeing that he was sincere and unspoiled. Ning Ken recollected going swimming with him at a reservoir that they called, with great satisfaction, their own Walden Pond.

In the winter of 1986, Wei An read Xu Chi's translation of Walden, *and the book changed his life. He discovered what he called Thoreau's "free, unrestrained, simple and open" organic style, and began composing in prose that, like Thoreau's, was poetic. He said the middle way fit him.*

As an American, I have an impulse to regard him as a naturalist, but his work resists this. For Wei An, the essence of Thoreau was not a "return to nature" but rather the "completion of man." Having grown up in the age of irony, I sometimes find it difficult to translate the unguarded expression of emotion and the direct discussion of truth, beauty, and goodness that are Wei An's idioms. His work reminds me, however, that our engagement with nature must necessarily be both romantic and scientific, and that the two cannot—or at least should not—be separated.

23

Bird trappers get going before first light and arrive in an orchard before the birds start flying. They set up three big nets in a triangle around a fruit tree.

On the tree's branches, they hang caged birds they have brought, and then hide themselves to wait. The bird trappers call the caged birds "decoys," and the decoys are there for their calls. Inside their cages the decoys turn around and around. Whenever they see wild birds flying by, the decoys flap their wings and call anxiously. Their miserable, sad cries make the wild birds turn back. Some of the wild birds hit the nets, others land in trees outside the nets, but after a while they too are drawn toward the cages. When the wild birds strike the nets, they fall down like leaves from a tree.

The Chinese painter and essayist Feng Zikai wrote that the old sheep used by shepherds to lead the flock to the slaughterhouse is considered a traitor to sheepkind. I will not say that the decoys are traitors to aviankind. Words like "traitor" should be used only in reference to humans.

34

I stumbled upon a beautiful spider in a northern woodlot. Its web was strung between two trees and was built from several parallel circular threads linked together by a few seemingly random radial threads. It was a big spider, with long, thin legs. Its body was unusually striking—light green alternating with orange. When I first came across it, I felt that flash of strong fear that is unlike the fear caused by any of the earth's other scary creatures. The same colors that are considered beautiful on one thing are horrifying and frightening on another.

37

There is a particular kind of beetle that you find on trees-of-heaven *(Ailanthus altissima),* also known as stinky toon trees. It is small, spotted, and shaped like an elephant. Biologists call it the elephant beetle, but country kids call it Old Mr. Lock. It likes to attach itself to the bark of the tree-of-heaven, sometimes quite low to the ground where one can reach out and grab it. But as soon as it's touched, no matter how gently, it quickly tucks in its six legs, tightly retracts its mouth—which is shaped like an elephant's trunk—and rolls up into a ball. When this happens, the children like to shout over and over, "Old Mr. Lock, Old Mr. Lock, open up and let us in!" They never get tired of shouting this, and they always sound completely sincere in their entreaties. As the saying goes, true sincerity can move mountains, and sooner or later the bugs relax, unroll, and then very carefully, like baby elephants, start to walk around on the children's palms.

41

Unlike other beginnings, the first big snowfall of the season always seems disorganized and unanticipated. Blessed by the first snowflakes of the year,

I wish to say, "Look at those country kids going to school for the very first time." Or, the first snowfall might be compared to the arrival of an unexpected guest. In welcoming this guest, the earth seems flustered and unprepared as it tries to deal with the surprise: things haven't been tidied up; the earth is just not ready to receive a guest. So while snow may be drifting through the air, the ground remains bare and inhospitable. As the snowflakes near the ground, they remind me of bees approaching the hive but not going in, or they remind me of the expatriates we read about in history books who wandered in exile, cut off from the land of their ancestors.

48

March is the month when travelers who make long journeys take to the road. Trips begin in March the way language begins with the urge to express oneself, and the way song begins with joy. In March even lambs are brave. The world is kind, and the road ahead is bright; the very stones are kind to our feet. A village in March is like a basket full of sunlight. Children race around while old folks sit against sunny walls. In March you want to work with your hands and your back, and the soil is like a young woman waiting on her wedding day. In March, our imaginations run away with us and we feel there is much before us, waiting to be done. In March, we are full of confidence, like travelers setting out on a long journey.

50

I once saw an American movie—I forget the name—that began this way: a boy who is bullied at school runs into a bookstore to hide, and he discovers, as if God had placed it there especially for him, a huge, magical book. The book tells the fairy tale of a big monster called The Nothing who is out to destroy a magical land called Fantasia. The boy enters and becomes part of the story. As the annihilation of Fantasia is imminent, and the queen is near death, the book says that the only way for them to be saved is for the boy to give the queen a brand-new name and to call out the name in a loud voice.

This movie and story have a very profound message. I'm reminded of Tagore's words: "Every child comes with the message that God is not discouraged of man."

58

One day in October, in an orchard near my home, the poet Hei Dachun had me and another friend play a fortune-telling game. It was a simple game. He began by telling us to each name the three animals we like best. I thought for a bit, then said sparrow, wild rabbit, and donkey (in general, I'm less fond of big, strong animals or brightly colored, beautiful ones than

I am of humbler, drab animals that are close to the earth). After we'd answered, Dachun said that the first animal you list is the person you love, the second animal is the one you think of as yourself, and the third animal is really you deep inside. It didn't bother me in the slightest that, according to the logic of this game, I am a donkey. I was happy to accept this.

When I got back home I got out a zoological dictionary and looked up *donkey* for the first time. The definition had a kind of literary quality: "The donkey is docile and endowed with great endurance; it can tolerate poor food and is more resistant to disease than other members of the family Equidae." As I was reading this, I remembered the praise the Spanish poet Juan Ramón Jiménez lavished on the donkey, which he called "patient and thoughtful, melancholic and lovable, the Marcus Aurelius of the fields."

59

Birds make different sorts of sounds. In the main, their voices can be divided into two categories that ornithologists refer to as "songs" and "calls." Songs, as the name implies, are primarily the sounds made by males in the spring to attract a mate. Calls, on the other hand, are more like speech, in that they are sounds birds use to exchange information. Songs are beautiful, emotional, expressive, beseeching, boastful. Calls are plain, descriptive, informative, communicative, commonplace. What must be understood is that the beautiful songs that most rend our hearts are not generally made by brightly colored birds, but by birds of the drabbest plumage. For example, both the skylark and the nightingale are dressed in attire that calls to mind the shabby clothes worn by the down-at-the-heels romantic poets, who so often wrote of these birds. This pairing of beautiful song with drab plumage is evidence of God's justice and an example of the deep mystery of life.

61

There is a certain bird whose song sounds like *gwa gwa gee,* and when I hear it, I always think of a troupe of itinerant folk balladeers. When summer comes and the reeds grow high in the marshes, the balladeers arrive from the south bringing their bamboo clappers with them. They live only by reed ponds, nowhere else, and they build their exquisite cup nests on reeds a meter or two above the surface of the water. Because there are fewer and fewer reed ponds to be found on our plains, their populations are, of course, in decline and it will be all too easy for them to slip toward extinction. In addition, their nests are a favorite target of cuckoos. When a cuckoo has laid its eggs in a nest, the mother bird cannot tell which eggs are her own and which are the cuckoo's. She has no way of knowing that the baby cuckoo she is feeding is eventually going to push her own babies out of the nest. Without suspicion, she will make countless trips back and forth from the nest in order to feed the bottomless hunger of this strange bird that is growing so much bigger than the other babies. The bird that I am writing about here has the beautiful Chinese name *weiying* (reed warbler) and is known in English as the paddyfield warbler. The likely fate of the paddyfield warbler is more heartbreaking than any of Shakespeare's tragedies.

74

Once I spent a night on Tianzi Mountain in Zhangjiajie, Hunan. In the evening I went for a walk by myself on a pitch-black mountain path, and when I heard the sound of water right next to me, I suddenly intuited the principle of correspondence between a river system and a country.

Just as any water course begins with a drop of water, human social grouping are formed only through the amalgamation of countless individuals. One drop of water, one person. When drops of water mingle joyfully to make a creek, a hamlet appears. Where several creeks flow together and make a stream, a village appears. And where several streams join and form a tributary big enough to be given a name, a county seat appears. And finally, when enough tributaries come together and form a river that flows to the sea, then you have provinces and a country. A country is like a watershed.

From an existential point of view, what does a single drop of water mean? It means death! This is why each drop of water at its formation contains within it true hope—the dream—that someday every drop of water on earth will merge into one. It is this wish that creates the great rivers which eventually give birth to the oceans. Since time immemorial, humans have had a similar wish. They want to rid themselves of boundaries, customs offices, and militaries, and to flow together into one big "ocean" of humanity. Today, this wish is still regarded as utopian.

Translation by Thomas Moran

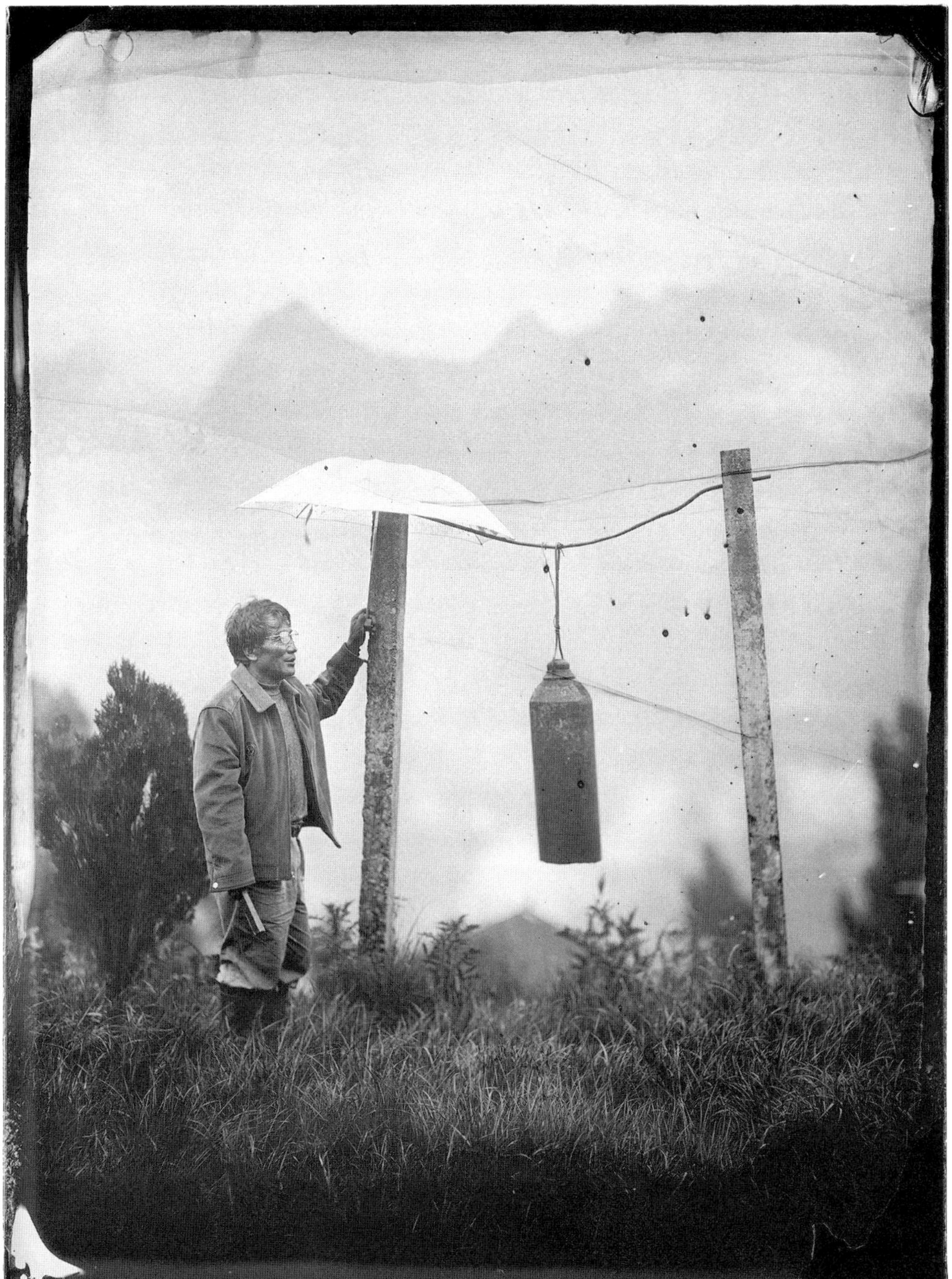

Luo Dan
Simple Song No. 25
John ringing the bell, Laomudeng Village
2010

庞 培

三首诗

云影

树在帮你呼吸
不被打扰地做完你的梦。河流、白云也是
清早，当你碰见一个好天气
你能从静静伫立的树身上
感觉到天色何其湛蓝，云影何等欢畅！
我们大家，我们全体
都被托在一枚树叶那么温凉
秋天的掌心

音乐

我抱着吉他。没有弹
想起一些人和事
一些数字
旧的会面
流逝的片断……
所有这些，比我可能弹奏的
音乐，更像是音乐
这是灵魂庞大的出席：
你十九岁，脸上有着
初涉人世的羞赧——

PANG PEI

Three Poems

CLOUD SHADOW

Trees are helping you to breathe
Unstirred, you finish your dream. Running river, clouds are also
morning, when you meet fine weather
you can feel from trees standing in silence
the joys of cloud shadows and such a blue sky!
All of us, the whole group,
are entrusted in a leaf, such cool
palm of autumn

MUSIC

I hug a guitar. Without playing it
thinking of some people and things
some numbers
old encounters
fading fragments . . .
All of these are more musical
than the music I can play
This is the massive attendance of soul:
you are nineteen, a shy face
that has just tasted the world—

雨中作

车厢在写诗
有一个人和一只手的扶手在写诗
刹车，绿灯
刮雨器写诗
叽叽嘎嘎的空座椅在写诗
雨落进黑夜
落入空无一人的站台
……这分行，空格的雨

COMPOSED IN THE RAIN

Writing a poem in a coach
A man and a hand help a hand to write a poem
It screeches to a halt, the light is green
Windshield wipers write a poem
A quaking empty seat is writing a poem
Rain falls into black night
into an empty platform
. . . this verse, a blank spacing of rain

Translations by Fiona Sze-Lorrain

张 枣

三首诗

哀歌

一封信打开有人说
天已凉
另一封信打开
是空的，是空的
却比世界沉重
一封信打开
有人说他在登高放歌
有人说，不，即便死了
那土豆里活着的惯性
还会长出小手呢
另一封信打开
你熟睡如橘
但有人剥开你的赤裸后说
他摸到了另一个你
另一封信打开
他们都在大笑
周身之物皆暴笑不已
一封信打开
行云流水在户外猖獗
一封信打开
我咀嚼着某些黑暗
另一封信打开
皓月当空
另一封信打开后喊
死，是一件真事情

1992

ZHANG ZAO

Three Poems

ELEGY

a letter opens and someone says
it's getting cold
another letter opens
it is empty, empty
yet heavier than the world
a letter opens
someone says he is singing from a mountain height
someone says *no, even if the potato was dead*
the inertia alive in it
would still grow tiny hands
another letter opens
you sleep like a tangerine
but after peeling off your nudity someone says
he has touched another you
another letter opens
they are all laughing
everything around explodes into laughter
a letter opens
clouds and water run wild outside
a letter opens
I am chewing a certain darkness
another letter opens
high moon in the sky
another letter opens and shouts
death is something real

(1992)

春秋来信

一

这个时辰的背面，才是我的家，
它在另一个城市里挂起了白旗。
天还没亮，睡眠的闸门放出几辆
载重卡车，它们恐龙般在拐口
撕抢某件东西，本就没有的东西。
我醒来。
　　　　　身上一颗绿口子滚落。

二

我们的绿扣子，永恒的小赘物。

云朵，砌建着上海。
　　　　　　　　　　我心中一幅蓝图
正等着增砖添瓦。我挪向亮处，
那儿，鹤，闪现了一下。你的信
立在室中央一柱阳光中理着羽毛——
是的，无需特赦。得从小白菜里，
从豌豆苗和冬瓜，找出那一个理解来，

来关掉肥胖和机器——
　　　　　　　　　　　我深深地
被你身上的矛盾吸引，移到窗前。
四月如此清澈，好似烈酒的反光，
街景颤抖着组合成深奥的比例。
是的，我喊不醒现实。而你的声音
追上我的目力所及："我，

就是你呀！我也漂在这个时辰里。
工地上就要爆破了，我在我这边
鸣这面锣示警。游过来呀，
接住这面锣，它就是你错过了的一切。"

三

我拾起地上的绿扣子，吹了吹。
开始忙我的事儿。
　　　　　　　　　静的时候，
窗下经过的邮差以为我是我的肖像；

LETTERS IN FOUR SEASONS

1

The obverse of this instant is indeed my home.
It raises a white flag in another city.
Before the crack of dawn, floodgates of sleep
let out some trucks. Like dinosaurs, at a turn
they claw for something which is nothing.
I wake up.
            A green button tumbles off my body.

2

Our green button, the tiny residue of eternity.

Clouds, bricking Shanghai.
                        A blueprint in my heart
awaits more brick and tile. I shift toward light.
There, a crane flashes for a second. Your letters
stand in a column of light at the center of the room, preening—
yes, no need for amnesty. Perception must be sought
inside *bok choy*, from pea shoots and winter melons.

Come, switch off obesity and machines—
                                        I'm deeply
drawn by contradictions on your body. Move over to the window.
Such a clear April, like light reflected off hard liquor.
Series of profound proportions shudder in street scenes.
Yes, my screams can't wake reality up. Yet your voice
catches the limits of my sight, *I—*

am you! I'm also drifting in this instant.
The construction site is going to explode. I'm right here
striking the gong to raise the alarm. Swim over here!
Catch this gong, it's everything you've missed.

3

I pick up a green button, and blow at it.
Start to busy myself with life.
                        In the stillness,
a postman passing by the window thinks I'm my portrait—

有时我趴在桌面昏昏欲睡，
双手伸进空间，像伸进一付镣铐，

哪儿，哪儿，是我们的精确呀？
　　　　　　　　　　　　　……绿扣子。

1997

世界

这个世界里还呈现另一个世界，
一个跟这个世界一模一样的
世界——不不，不是另一个而是
同一个。是一个同时也是两个

世界。
　　　因而我信赖那看不见的一切。
夜已深，我坐在封闭的机场，
往你没有的杯中
倾倒烈酒。
　　　　　没有的燕子的脸。
正因为你戴着别人的
戒指，
我们才得以如此亲近。

sometimes I sluggishly sprawl across the table,
both hands reaching into emptiness, like reaching into a pair
    of handcuffs.

Where, where is our precision?
                                        … Green button.

(1997)

WORLD

Yet another world emerges in this world.
A world just like this one
world—no, no, not another but
the same one. One and two

worlds.
        This is why I trust all that stays invisible.
Late at night, I sat at the closed airport,
pouring hard liquor into
your empty glass.
                    No sparrow's face.
Because you were wearing someone else's
ring,
we became so intimate.

Translations by Fiona Sze-Lorrain

杨 子

三首诗

巨大的车间

我以为只有我一个，
在密室里，在峭壁上
写着古怪的句子。
往四周一看，
才发现我是在一个巨大的车间里，
那么多人埋头在书桌上，
犹如裁缝埋头在缝纫机上，
辛辛苦苦，字斟句酌，
废寝忘食，磨铁成针。
我看到更多的车间，更多的人，
每个人的身边
都有一个麻袋，
有人从里边拿出卡夫卡，博尔赫斯，卡尔维诺，
有人从里边拿出《奥义书》《伪经》或者六十四卦，
有人从里边拿出女人的一绺青发或者孔雀蓝的亵衣，
有人从里边拿出干抹布一样皱巴巴的梦，
有人从里边拿出父亲的书信祖父的照片曾祖的遗言，
有人寒冬腊月穿着小背心，
有人大热天套着老棉鞋，
有人耳朵上夹根烟，
有人钱包里放避孕套，
有人不停地发短信
给折磨他的小妖精。
五分钟
或者一辈子，
他们完成那么多分行文字，
押韵或者不押韵，
抒情或者反抒情，
他们把它叫做诗，
靠它活命万万不能，
但是如果你把它夺去，
扔到阴沟里，
那会要了他们的命，

YANG ZI

Three Poems

GIANT WORKPLANT

I thought I was the only one
in a back room, on a cliff,
writing odd phrases.
Looking around,
I realized I was in a giant workplant,
where so many were buried in work at their writing desks,
like tailors buried in work at sewing machines,
laboriously, weighing every word,
meals forgotten, little strokes felling great oaks.
I saw more workplants, more men,
each with a sack
by his side.
Someone took out Kafka, Borges, Calvino.
Someone took out the *Upanishads*, the *Pseudepigrapha*
    or the sixty-four hexagrams.
Someone took out a lock of green woman's hair or the blue
    underwear of a peacock.
Someone took out dreams wrinkled like rags.
Someone took out his father's letter grandfather's photograph
    great-grandfather's testament.
Someone wore a singlet in the dead of winter.
Someone put on old cotton shoes on a hot day.
Someone stuck a cigarette behind his ear.
Someone put condoms in his wallet.
Someone kept sending short messages
to the little vixen torturing him.
Five minutes
or a lifetime,
they completed so many verses.
Rhyming or not,
lyrical or not,
they called it poetry.
Impossible to rely on it for a living.

他们会一起高喊，
吓死你。

悲痛的星辰

今夜，那些悲痛的星辰
都要开口说话。

所有死去的屋子里
都有人活着，

嘴里喷出黑药丸的气息，
无处申告的哀痛的气息。

那些暗哑的星辰！
那些燃烧的星辰！

都要开口，
都要痛斥，

为了让活着的死人醒来！
为了让无边的厄运崩溃！

铁灰色天空

铁灰色的天空像一座传染病院，
所有人都被它吸进去，
所有痴呆的，狡黠的人，
所有面相善良，面相凶恶的人，
所有不想离开，不愿留下的人，
都被它吸进去，
吸进去。

寂静中，
飞鸟像一块石头，
笔直地砸在后院，
发出嗡嗡的响声。

妇女在家中准备晚餐。
她已经没有了姣好的身材，

Yet if you snatched it,
threw it into a drain,
it'd kill them.
They'd yell together,
scaring you to death.

GRIEVING STARS

Tonight, all those sorrowful stars
open their mouths and speak.

In all dead houses,
the living

spurt out the breath of black pills from their mouths,
mournful breath with nowhere to lodge complaints.

Muffled stars!
Burning stars!

Opening their mouths.
Lashing out.

To awaken the living dead!
To ruin the edgeless doom!

STEEL GRAY SKY

Steel gray sky like a contagious hospital—
all the people are sucked into it,
all senile, cunning people
all kind-looking, ferocious-looking people,
all those who do not wish to leave or stay,
are sucked into it,
sucked.

In stillness,
a flying bird is like a stone
hit straight into the courtyard,
buzzing loudly.

A woman is preparing dinner at home.
She no longer has a slender figure.

她已经没有了从前的骄傲。
窗外一股沁凉的甜蜜气味，
可能是玉兰花，
也可能是刚刚诞生的
某种无名疾病。
她毫无知觉，
依旧忙碌。
猪肉，洋葱，
皮蛋，料酒，
米饭煮上了，
锅里炖着腰子。

铁灰色的天空，
把千家万户的灯盏
压到腐臭的渠沟里。

成堆的病人哪儿去了，
那些不想离开，不愿留下的人？
天空何时变成可怕的烧焦的黑色？
在她拍打过冬的被褥和发霉的枕头的时候？
在她给肉汤加入茴香和胡椒的时候？

她的鼻子已经很迟钝了，
无论窗外甜丝丝阴沉沉的威胁，
还是过道里飘来的
邻居冒着热气的幸福，
她都毫无知觉。
她放更多的盐，更多的辣椒。
她望着"家庭录像"里摔个狗吃屎的男子
和四脚朝天的儿童，
笑不起来。

她想，丈夫正在回家的路上。
是的，正在回家的路上，
一个女孩在电话里哭喊，
"我肚子疼，你来!"
"我想来，来不了!"
他的回答带着一丝哭腔，
他的脚步比铅还要沉重。
这是意志昏沉的时间，
这是幽灵侵袭的时间。

她看见一扇扇亮起灯光的窗户，
远的，像银子的碎屑，
近的，像矩形的白金钻戒，

She no longer has the pride from the past.
A delicious honey fragrance blows from the window—
perhaps magnolia
or the newly born
so-and-so disease.
Unwittingly, she
busies herself as usual.
Pork, onions,
century eggs, cooking wine,
rice is ready,
pig kidneys are stewed in a pot.

Steel gray sky,
pressing lamps of thousands of families
into a pungent trench.

Where are the stacks of patients—
those who do not wish to leave or stay?
When did the sky turn into a frightful, burnt black?
When she was beating winter bedding and moldy pillows?
When she was adding fennel and pepper to meat soup?

Her nose is already musty.
Regardless of the sweetly dark menace outside,
or the steam of bliss from neighbors
drifting from the corridor,
she senses nothing.
She adds more salt, more chili pepper.
She stares at a man eating dog shit during a "family video" program,
and children upside-down,
but can't bring herself to laugh.

She reckons, *Hubby is on the way home.*
Yes, on the way home,
a girl is crying over the phone,
"Come, my stomach is aching!"
"I want to come, but I can't!"
His answer carries a mournful tune,
his footsteps heavier than lead.
This is the moment of muddled will,
the moment for spirits to invade.

She sees lamps light up window by window,
afar, like pieces of silver,
nearby, like rectangular diamond rings in platinum,

漂浮在黑夜宽阔的渠沟中，
犹如博览会上的婚戒陈列部。

她听见上楼的脚步声了，
很沉重，
仿佛一个疝气患者。
她没有准备笑容。
她想，她也不会见到他的笑容。
在哭丧着脸的铁灰色天空中浸泡了一天之后，
他们的表情都像是医院里等待确诊的病人。
但是无论如何，
这是他，
回来了。
他们可以一起平躺在大床上，
犹如平躺在黑色的天空，
忘记对光明的爱和盼望
给他们带来如此多的屈辱。

drifting in the wide trench of black night,
like a display of wedding rings at an exhibition.

She hears footsteps upstairs,
very heavy,
like a hernia patient.
She has not prepared a smile.
She reckons, she'll never see his smile.
After soaking a day in the wailing sky,
they look like patients waiting to be diagnosed in a hospital.
But no matter how,
it is him
returning home.
They can lie together on a huge bed,
like lying in black sky,
forgetting how their love and yearning for light
have brought them so much humiliation.

Translations by Fiona Sze-Lorrain

The Source and the Bird

Translator's Note

In contemporary Chinese history, very few literary figures are revered as much as Hai Zi, a poet who has become a cult figure. He was twenty-five when he committed suicide, in 1989, by lying in the path of a train that ran between Shanhaiguan and Longjiagong. Hai Zi had with him four books: the Old and New Testament, the short stories of Joseph Conrad, Kon-Tiki, *and* Walden.

Hai Zi's name, literally translated, means "son, or boy, of the sea." He admired Hölderlin and the European Romantic poets, such as Byron, and a central theme in his work is the self-sacrifice of the poet, who is martyred by his art. In Hai Zi's poems, one feels a cosmic harmony: sorrowful yet soothing, natural yet shrouded. Despite the acute desire for death he expressed in his writing, Hai Zi also wrote tender, sensuous prose and poetry, reflecting on the seasons, nature, the beauty of light, and the sorrows of love. His style is figurative and economic rather than rhetorical, though he often refers to epics, myths, histories, and legends.

When translating Hai Zi, I am cautious to avoid a psychological reading, to keep a distance from the schizophrenic tendencies in his work, and from his personal darkness. I am more interested in the mystery in his images, the narrative drive and the music: through them, I travel faster, lighter, and farther.

In the upper river course, a little path leading to the mountain peak blossoms with red flowers that glow like fresh blood. Rotting tree leaves are hooded with a layer of water, as if yearning for firelight and love. Thick silhouettes emerge from tree caves and grottoes. The lakes have flooded half the mountain and forests. Hope and blessing arrive in this mortal world. Crimson herds of horses speed by. A tribe from nowhere is wandering about. The indistinct, snow-capped mountaintop and grass slopes starkly contrast the ugliness of mankind. Men use their dense eyelashes to blind themselves to the rainy season behind their eyes. From beneath their festive life, an immensely painful memory is seeping. Impoverished mountain. Where are we from? Where are we going? Who are we? As we cross over the night, a red moon and one or two radiant musical instruments, polished by hands and lips, keep us company. That red moon is like a huge, indelible birthmark. On a July evening, I cannot stay silent anymore, and send in agony a story to each basket of fire. About a mother who was wakened in the middle of the night by the kicking legs of the child inside her, tangled in its umbilical cord. About a lover whose hair was burned into curls by my respiration, and settled over the soft chest. About seeds in the snow and sorrow of the North. About friendship and the blood-soaked shield. About shooting stars that fall and fly back up to the sky. About *Eupatorium fortunei* and lilies-of-the-valley, about the weeping of a bride. About a bloodstained palm of a hand that bears animosity. About righteousness, prayer, and revenge. About the just sunshine that strikes a criminal's naked back like a whip. About a pastoral song and the moon goddess. Many wake up, then fall asleep again. Many fall asleep, then wake up. By the fire, shadows become an enormous mass. Finally, I speak of the bird. Full of wit. Flying cannot be surpassed. Flight cannot be solved by physical strength and intelligence. It is a miracle. If you would stride into the birds' way, you would feel lonely. Your heart expands and contracts under the warm feathers. Your heart is born not for defense but to fly. The guns at ground level take aim at you. In that intensely blue yet sad sky you fly with a chest packed with seeds, and you fly on, lonely, bitter, your companion a hatred toward the profane world.

(1983)

Translation by Fiona Sze-Lorrain

阿 芒

兩首詩

我緊緊抱你的時候這世界好多人死

我緊緊抱你的時候這世界好多人餓死
我緊緊抱你的時候這世界好多人戰死
我緊緊抱你的時候這世界好多人發生意外，死了
我緊緊抱你的時候這世界好多人自己幫助自己死去，環抱自己的手一下子
　放鬆
我不抱世界這麼多沒有呼吸了的人我抱你就抱著感覺窒息在我緊緊
也被你緊緊地抱住這時候這麼多人感覺不到
我們
瀕臨真空拔高的愛情的顫抖
潮浪
越過了石堆
那麼多現在不動聲色
被搬動的石頭
下一刻
愛
能不能
下一刻
更多不動
被搬動的石頭
沒有答案
不要
有
我知道我們能不能再互相緊緊抱著是我不知道的
或者在某個人停下來想下一個字
一顆炮彈在空中優美地畫過
一滴水飽滿地騰越
潛水艇安安靜靜
地雷乖巧
掃乾淨的地灰塵爭相落下
草籽兒精神好綠
你也感覺到了嗎在你緊緊抱我的時候好多人死了

AMANG

Two Poems

SO MANY PEOPLE DIE
WHILE I'M HUGGING YOU TIGHTLY

so many people starve to death while I'm hugging you tightly
so many people war to death while I'm hugging you tightly
so many people have accidents, die while I'm hugging you tightly
so many people help themselves to death, hands that encircle them
    suddenly relax, while I'm hugging you tightly
I don't hug so many people who don't breathe I hug you like
    suffocation I tightly hug tightly hugged by you while so many
    people can't feel
us
the shudder of love at a height close to a vacuum
tides
over rocks
so many rocks that are now
moved in silence
in the next moment
love
can't even
stay more immobile
in the next moment
rocks that are moved
have no answer
no
yes
I know can't we hug each other tightly I don't know
or a person who stops to think about a word
a bomb beautifully tracing a line in the sky
a drop of water heartily soaring over
submarines stay quiet
land mines stay obedient
dust competes to fall on the cleanly swept floor
grass seeds in such green spirits

你緊緊抱我的時候好多人精神錯亂走過熄滅篝火旁歪歪倒倒營帳深深淺淺
　石堆
好多人流星飛過我們接著吻的窗臺
你聽得到窗外的鳥
蟬
那麼多
比石器時代更久遠的石頭？

懷疑

有一刻我懷疑她們全死了。
沒有「倖存者」
「Survivor」
我甚至懷疑「倖存者」根本是翻譯來的，一場外來雨
落進乾燥多隙縫的土地
這兒沒這個用法
也不需要這個詞：
我們的人太多
太多
就是說沒什麼特別的不幸
滄海桑田，全球暖化，命運，出生地，外來物種，XYZ
廚房，餐廳，後院
宗教，文化，倫理
別人的房間
自己的房間
蒙面俠
強姦犯
小偷
駭客
沒錯有些人看起來像通過困難的地形
有些人聽起來像經歷奇妙的地理區域
有些人感覺起來有如
穿越了時間
但在這一刻
我打下這些字的時間
你讀到這些字的時間
她們
活著嗎
全部？
某些？
少數？
半個？

can you also feel it so many people die while I'm hugging you tightly
while you're hugging me tightly so many people go crazy walk
    through smothered bonfire swaying tents deep and shallow
    stacks of rocks
so many shooting stars fly past the windowsill we've kissed
can you hear the birds outside
cicadas
so many rocks
more ancient than those from the Stone Age?

DOUBT

for a moment I doubt if they are all dead
no *xingcunzhe*
survivor
I even doubt if *xingcunzhe* is actually a translation, a foreign rain
falling into the parched cracked land
we don't need such usage
or this noun here:
there are too many of us
too many
which means no particular misfortune
the world changes with time, global warming, destiny, place of birth,
    foreign species, XYZ
kitchen, canteen, courtyard
religion, culture, ethics
rooms of others
a room of one's own
masked swordsman
rapist
thief
hacker
indeed some people seem as if they're passing through a difficult
    topography
some people sound as if they've experienced a marvelous
    geographical region
some people feel like
penetrating time
but at this moment
when I'm typing these words
when you're reading these words
are they
alive
all?

沒有？
她們如何逃過劫數
那一次和後來的幾次
還有未來
一直一直來……
不只一刻我懷疑
但她們繼續
像死去的星星
穿透天空和時間
還是那麼亮
那麼動人
還是引發了波瀾和災難
某種不朽
垃圾
詩和歌

some?
half?
none?
how did they scrape through
that one time and the next few times
and in the future
until until . . .
for more than a moment I doubt
but they continue
like dead stars
penetrating sky and time
still so bright
so moving
still initiating waves and disasters
a certain longevity
rubbish
poetry and song

Translations by Fiona Sze-Lorrain

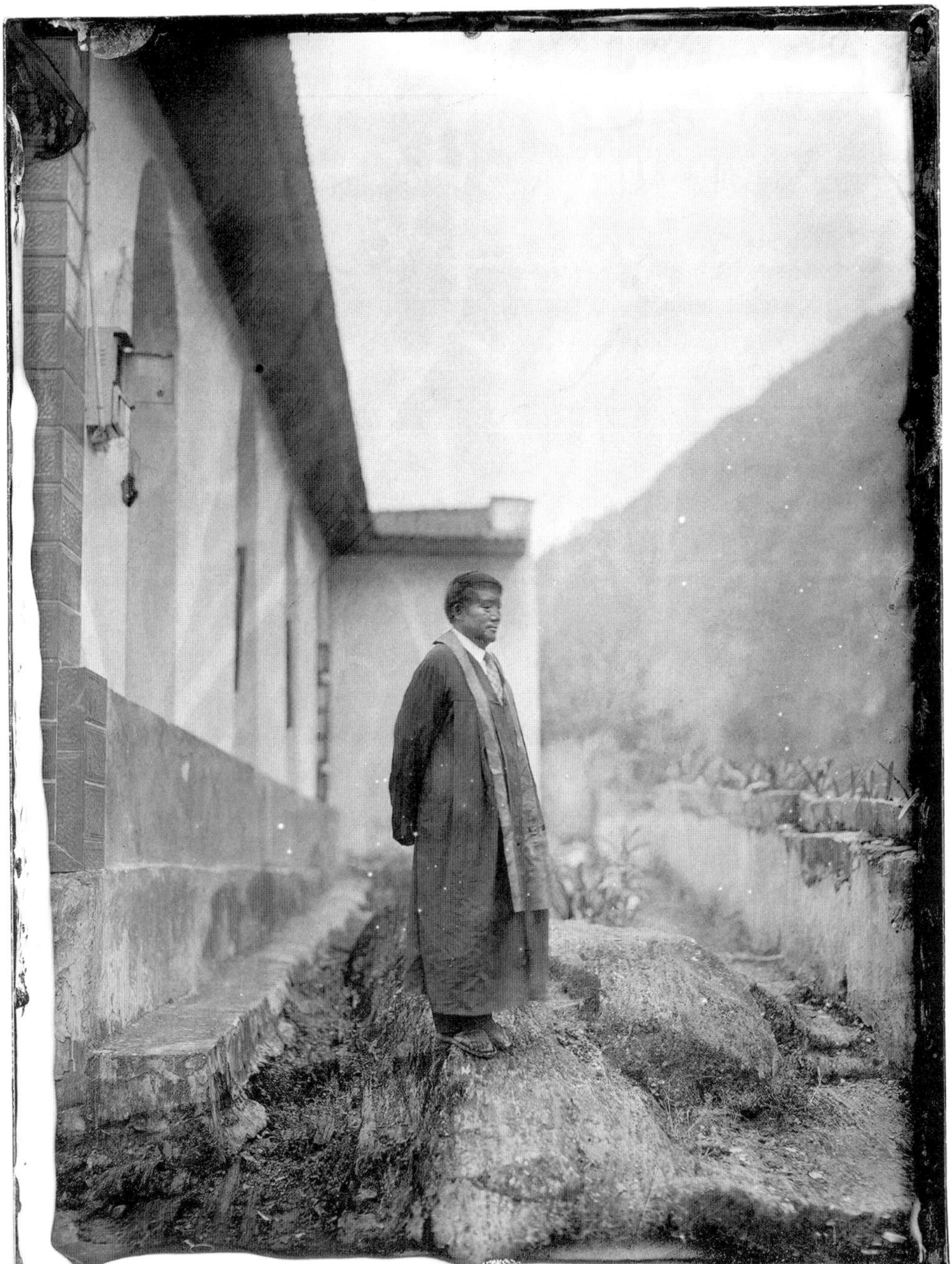

Luo Dan
Simple Song No. 8
Sang Lusi, a pastor of the Bible Training School, Munima Village
2010

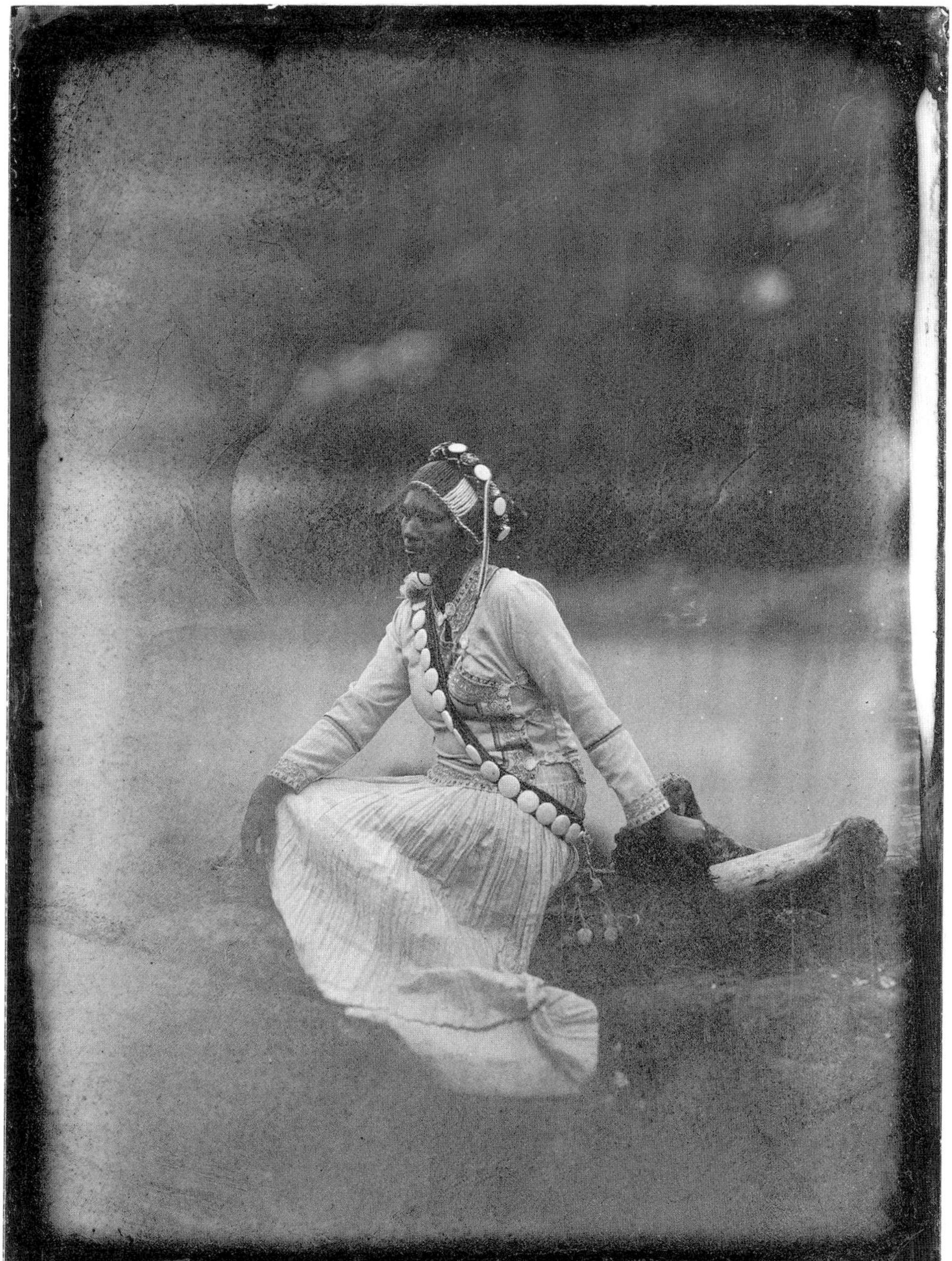

Luo Dan
Simple Song No. 19
Qia Fusheng, Shidi Village
2010

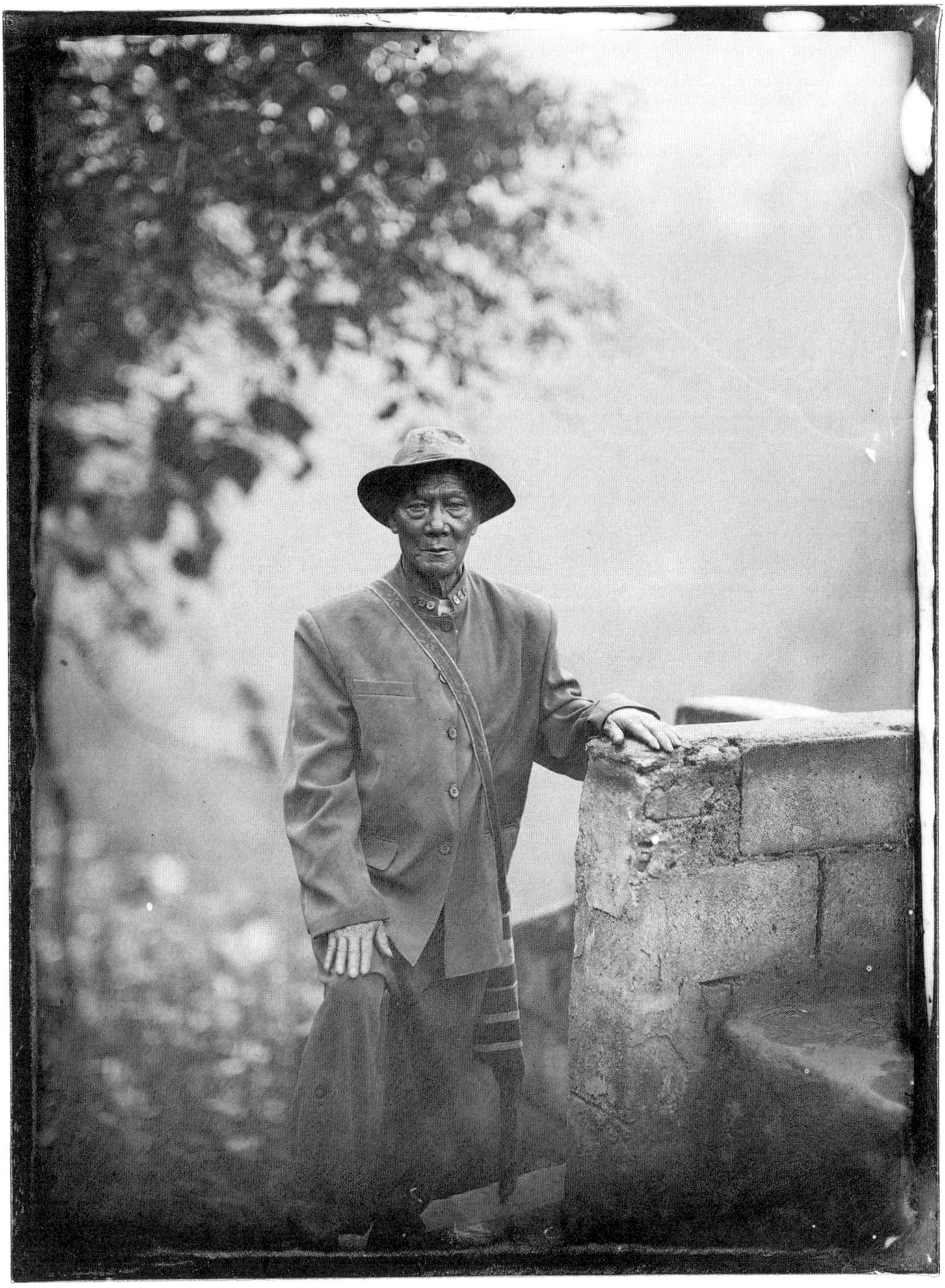

Luo Dan
Simple Song No. 27
Pu Aqi, Shimendeng Village
2010

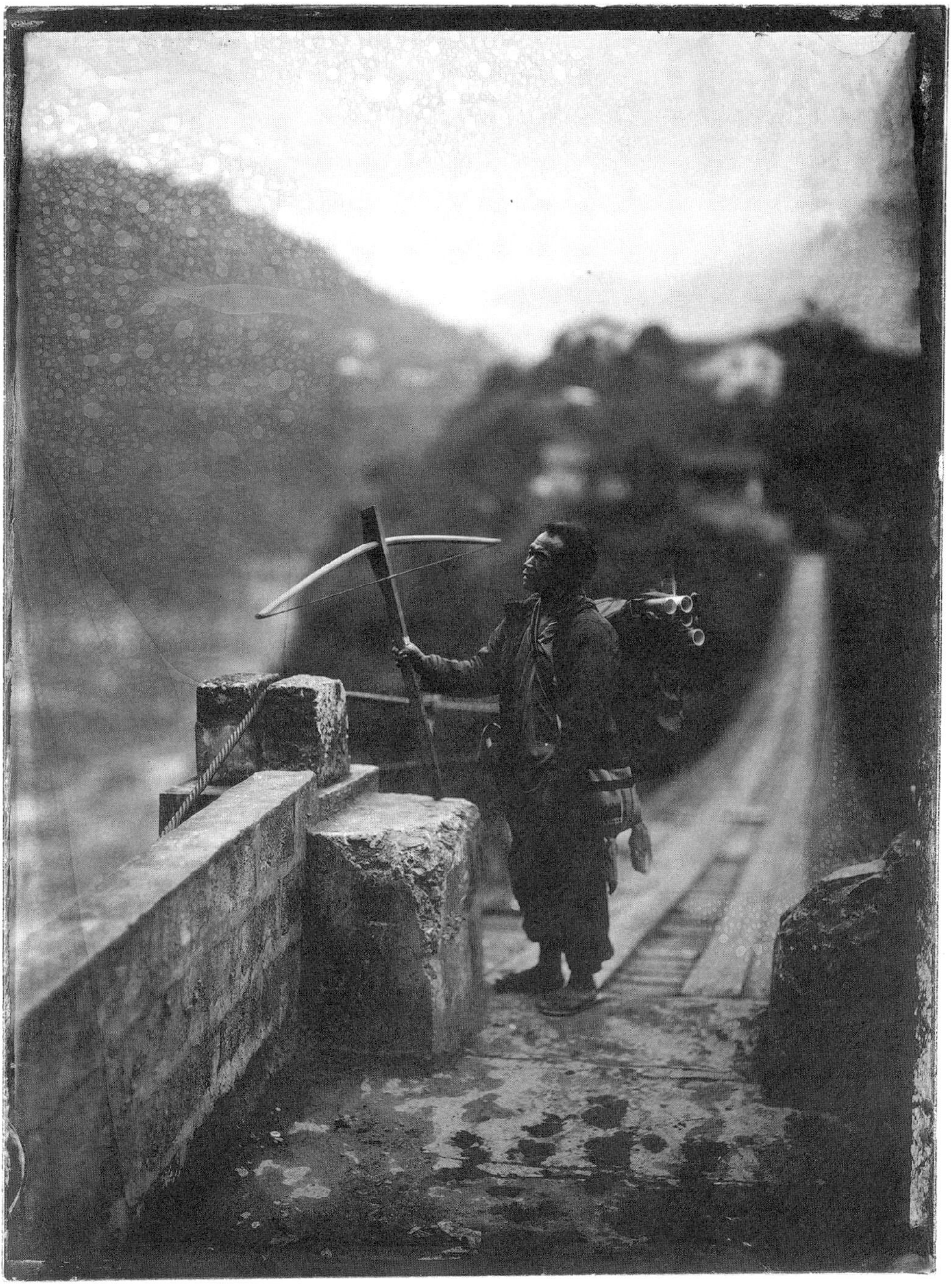

Luo Dan
Simple Song No. 28
Sha Yihai with crossbow, Shidi Village
2010

Rinchen, the Sky-Burial Master

Anyone writing about a sky-burial master is sure to be suspected of having chosen a sensational subject just to get attention. When one brings up sky burials, all kinds of exotic stereotypes about Tibet leap to mind. Then, if one mentions a sky-burial master, one imagines a uniquely Tibetan practitioner, whose profession involves something between a weird science of dissection and witchcraft. The photographs of sky-burial masters that can be found easily on the Internet don't reveal much information. For example, there are well-known images from the 1980s, taken at the sky-burial site near Lhasa's Sera Monastery. In one of the photographs, a solemn-looking Tibetan man is holding a broad-bladed knife and standing over a tangle of body parts; the bloody flesh only vaguely resembles a human corpse. The scene looks like a bizarre, open-air surgery. Anyone with a sensitive nature would be thoroughly shocked by the images.

The friend who sent me the links to those photographs is a poet who has traveled to Tibet many times, even though he is from south of the Yangtze River. He asked me a little nervously, "Is it possible that all you Tibetans want burials like that when you die?"

Actually, I had to think hard about how to answer him, because it's not something that can be explained in just a few sentences. It's fairly simple, of course, to describe in a literal way what happens at a traditional sky burial, and many of those kinds of descriptions have been written. There is even a well-known poem that praises the vultures that eat the corpses ... You can imagine the thrill that people with romanticized ideas about Tibetans get when they read such things. For them, the knife-wielding sky-burial master has the aura of a mystical person with the power to unite the opposing cosmic principles of *yin* and *yang*. In reality, though, being a sky-burial master is not something that just anyone would want to do or could do. To be a sky-burial master you need the courage to bloody your hands with the harsh evidence of life's impermanence, without ever losing your sense of deep compassion.

In Tibet or, more accurately, in all Tibetan areas—it is necessary to make this distinction so readers will not think I mean only the official Tibetan Autonomous Region—a sky-burial master is simply a layperson in one's hometown who helps people on their way to reincarnation. His skills and tools are the same as a butcher's, so he has a low social status despite being someone whom everyone needs and comes into contact with eventually. When we die, we need lamas, but we also need a *tokden* [Tibetan for sky-burial master].

I remember the time I was staying in Palyul, in Baiyu County. Every morning I would get up early and go to the beautiful Palyul Monastery, built against the base of the mountain, and stay there until dusk. In fact, I was there so often that I almost became the full-time cook for Karma Kuchen Rinpoche, the current Throne Holder of the Palyul Lineage. My culinary skills aren't that great, but I can cook up a pretty good dish of potatoes and beef. You just need to have the courage to throw in lots of chili, Sichuan peppers, and other spices, then heat them all together in a big pot. After a while, you have a really spicy and fragrant dish. I like to tell myself that even now the *draba* [ordinary monks] and Karma Kuchen Rinpoche cherish the memory of me as the person who always made their mouths burn.

When I was at Dabpa County's Bangpu Monastery, instead of being the cook, I took cooking lessons from Drongkar. You would never imagine that a monk could make such amazing steamed buns: very big and white, and delicious with butter tea. The *tsampa* that Drongkar rolled was even better than his steamed buns. In Lhasa, the barley flour for *tsampa* is ground very fine, using water-powered millstones or machines. But in Kham, the barley flour is ground by hand, so it's coarser. As a result, Kham's *tsampa* has a stronger barley taste.

The day I departed from Bangpu Monastery, with the intention of going to Dartsedo, Drongkar saw me waiting for the bus on the main road near the monastery. As he was helping me load my backpack, he stuffed some things into my pocket. I tried to see what they were, but he insisted that I not look until I had left. After a while, when the bus was some distance down the road, I reached in my pocket and saw that he had given me *chinden* [Tibetan Buddhist medicine]. I tried to look back at the maroon walls of the monastery, but they had disappeared from view. I felt around in my pocket again and discovered that Drongkar had also given me a 50 RMB note [Chinese currency]. I almost cried. I knew that he was poor, and his gift showed how wholeheartedly he wanted me to become a true pilgrim.

The bus took me to Nyakchuka. My reason for traveling there was related to a letter from Chodrak, a person in Nyakchuka who had written to me about meeting an authentic sky-burial master. Those few sentences had piqued my curiosity. (You should notice that my stopover in Nyakchuka, en route to Dartsedo, shows how frugal and practical I am when I travel, stopping wherever I please—in the true spirit of "on the road.") I discovered that Chodrak was tall, handsome, and youthful, with curly hair and black eyes. "Do you want to get to know Tokden Rinchen? I can take you to see him," he asked me shortly after we met. "A *tokden?* What's so special about that?" I replied. "I didn't travel all the way from Lhasa to Kham to see a *tokden*. Lhasa has plenty of *tokden*. What do you take me for," I added somewhat brusquely, "one of those inland-China types who come to Tibet to see exotic, occult things?" Chodrak simply smiled. "This *tokden* is not like any you've ever met; he's a civil servant, head of the livestock protection department."

Eventually, Chodrak and I traveled to the Horra grasslands, and to the livestock disease prevention office—actually just a small lodge—where Tokden Rinchen worked. I have a keen sense of smell, and when Rinchen came in, cordially bringing me a nice hot cup of butter tea, I noticed his peculiar odour. I can't say for sure that all sky-burial masters have this scent. In any case, I had no choice but to take the tea and to make small talk. I had noticed a portrait of Chairman Mao hanging on the wall. It was the familiar portrait that we'd all grown up with. Next to Rinchen's bed was a small wooden box covered by a thin felt cloth and draped with a *khata* [traditional ceremonial scarf]. On the box was a figure of Shakyamuni [the historical Buddha]. Next to the figure was an offering of two freshly plucked wildflowers.

"Rinchen," I asked, "what exactly do you believe in?" I knew the question was complicated, and his answer surprised me. "During the day," he said, "I believe in Chairman Mao; once the sun goes down, I believe in our Bodhisattvas." I gave him a perplexed look, then he burst out laughing, proud of himself for having teased me. His joke made me forget about the cup of butter tea I had cautiously put on the table without tasting. I was still wrestling with the fact that the tea had been made by a sky-burial master. (But wait, I'm getting way ahead of myself in telling the story of how I met Rinchen.)

In Nyakchuka, Chodrak had been the head of the county religious affairs bureau, and I never imagined that one day he would become the head of the county tourism bureau. Actually, the tourism industry suited him. I should mention that it was thanks to me—someone who loves to travel—that he first considered tourism as a career. I have always had great interest in this region of the country, so it's very possible that my admiration and excitement renewed his strong feelings about his native land. The prospect of expressing his heartfelt love for the place, and extending his genuine sense of hospitality, may have influenced him, along with the realization that tourism could generate income for the people while preserving the region's many natural resources. Of course, I was never the kind of traveler that generated any income for them (on the contrary, they spent a lot of money on me), but I think I helped inspire them.

Chodrak said he was the lowest official among the low-ranking officials. Even so, arranging for horses to be brought from town for us wasn't a problem. Well, there was a slight problem. Usually, Chodrak could just give orders over the phone to have horses sent. However, my visit to Nyakchuka coincided with the season for a local activity even more lucrative than tourism—gathering mushrooms. When I arrived, none of the village's government workers were at their posts. One by one they had all run off to look for mushrooms. Not a single official in the village was answering his phone. Chodrak threw up his hands and had no choice but to dispatch one of his staff on horseback to carry his message. This turned out to be effective. Apparently, in rural Tibetan areas, things still work best the old-fashioned way.

Three workers promptly arrived with horses for us. In addition to the workers, the trip to Horra would include Chodrak, me, and an exemplary "teacher of the people" named Tenzin. But what kind of official work could Chodrak say our group would be doing out on the grasslands? Without hesitation, Chodrak announced that we would be conducting research into a monastery in the town. Tenzin added that the township had a small school that was incomplete and needed to be inspected. But why was I coming along? With my two cameras hanging around my neck, everyone always assumed that I was a "journalist," so without further questions I had a justification for being part of the group. In reality, of course, Chodrak and Tenzin were accompanying me to meet Tokden Rinchen.

I never thought the journey to meet Rinchen would be so lengthy. I only gradually came to realize the difficulty after I had been riding for some time on the back of a big horse, my saddlebags overstuffed with all kinds of junk. (I should mention that this junk included my backpack, which contained my sleeping bag, tape recorder and rolls of tape, film, my make-up and toiletries, and so forth. The other stuff in the saddle bags were quilts and overcoats, which were the only personal items that Chodrak and Tenzin took on the trip.) Chodrak's and Tenzin's horses carried our food supplies and a rice cooker. (For the record, I want to mention that we bought all these things ourselves and did not use any public funds; Chodrak and his colleagues never wanted to create the appearance that they were sponging off the people's money.)

We were riding our horses through a place where lotus flowers were in full bloom, when Chodrak and Tenzin stopped. Saying they were "going to look for mushrooms," they left me with Tashi, the horse keeper, and disappeared into the woods. Tashi took the horses to graze nearby, and I lay down among the flowers. Against the meadow of wild grasses, the colorful flowers created the appearance of a brightly woven rug. I had the urge to burst into song in praise of Kham's amazing beauty. I'd never felt such a strong urge to sing—and have never felt that way since. Unfortunately, I didn't know any songs capable of expressing the beauty around me. On top of that, even if I had thought of an appropriate song, my voice isn't good enough. I could not have done justice to either the song or the beauty. I realized that I was a Tibetan who had been estranged from the natural landscape for too long. Tashi, on the other hand, simply burst into song, and I couldn't get enough of his singing. What a wonderful voice he had.

When we were all riding together and Tashi wasn't singing, I liked listening to my taped music. I slipped my sore feet out of the stirrups and let them dangle alongside the horse's belly. Because I didn't feel like talking, I deliberately rode behind everyone else. I just enjoyed listening through my earphones to the slow chanting of an old lama who had been a hermit for many years, and the gentle rocking of the horse. Wherever I looked, the land was beautiful. Then suddenly the horses started getting jittery, raising their heads and looking from side to side. I leaned low and caught sight of a slender snake swiftly disappearing into the grass. Actually, I didn't see very much of anything before I was thrown off my horse and hit my head on a rock. My companions, riding in front, heard me shriek. They turned and hurriedly galloped back. In my head was the chanting of the lama's soft mantra, but it didn't lessen the pain of hitting the ground. I immediately began to cry . . .

(Hey, hold on! I can't get off track and start talking about myself. I'm writing about Rinchen!)

After we had ridden over several mountains, crossed several rivers, and at last reached the Horra County government office (where we slept on the floor), did we finally meet Rinchen, the sky-burial master. People say his home pastures are very far from the county office, and so when we arrived, Chodrak once again had to send messengers on horseback. When I first saw Rinchen, his brow was beaded with sweat, and his hands held the reins of an exhausted horse he was pulling along behind him. He had been tending to a sick cow and had been in the middle of giving it an injection when he received our message. He had immediately gotten on his horse and ridden fast for over six hours. I felt a bit ashamed. After all, he wasn't the one who had wanted to meet. How could I rudely bother him in this manner?

But Rinchen's face was joyous when he saw Chodrak, as though he was seeing his own son. They had known each other for many years and had a firm friendship. Chodrak not only drank the tea Rinchen made, but also ate his yogurt. Whenever Rinchen had to take part in a county livestock protection meeting away from Horra, he would stay in Chodrak's home. This kind of companionship was unusual. As head of the livestock protection department, Rinchen had the rank of a government official, but he was still widely regarded as a *tokden*. It's true that people depend on the *tokden* to be there after they die, but while they're alive, they more or less avoid him. *Tokdens* have a strange air about them, but Chodrak was a close friend nonetheless.

I was still puzzling over Rinchen's odor as he stood before me with his long, curly black hair and weather-beaten face. His thick body was bundled up in a military-green overcoat, his feet were squeezed into felt boots, and he walked with a limp, like many nomads who ride horses from the time they are very small. Almost sixty years old, he remarked that pretty soon he himself would need a *tokden*.

As we mounted up and headed toward the sky-burial ground, I once again let my horse trail the others. Up ahead, Rinchen and Chodrak were laughing and joking. In the distance I could see the sky-burial ground and could smell its unusual odour on the light breeze. In truth, it was the scent of death. When we were right upon it, the sky-burial ground looked pretty much like the surrounding area. When you looked carefully, however, you could see the bloodstains spattered here and there, and notice where the grass seemed flattened and thin. There was also an abundance of insects.

We dismounted at a spot where the scent of death was strongest, and Rinchen's demeanor suddenly changed. He became very professional . . .

"Let me start by talking about the *feng shui* of the sky-burial site," he said. "This area was not just selected at random; a long time ago it was chosen by a lama. Take a good look at the site. Do you see how it resembles a raft? It is in fact a kind of raft. All kinds of corpses are brought here: male, female, old, young. Some are also monks. Mostly they are carried from the surrounding villages. But there is a limit to the number of corpses that can be brought to this sky-burial ground. If there are too many corpses, then ghosts will appear. Like a raft, a sky-burial site can't hold everyone. I don't know how many years this site has been in use, only that it's been here for a long time. I have been a *tokden* for over twenty years now, and I've used the knife on over two hundred dead people. How many passed through here before I came? When I look around, I don't see enough space for too many more."

Rinchen took me by the arm, pointed to the grass under our feet, and squinted his eyes, as though he were trying to get me to look at all the dead people around us. But how could I be expected to see them? I became flustered and rose up on my tiptoes.

"If the dead are not given a good sky burial, they can become like the very scary ghosts painted in traditional murals: skeletons hovering over burial sites. I have never seen ghosts, but maybe the scent of death is so much on me that even the ghosts are repelled. In any case, plenty of other people have seen ghosts. Recently a young female herder saw them.

"Unless they have died a violent death, most people here are given a sky burial. Others are sent to Horlung for sky burial. The burial site there is located on a hillside and is very big. All Lithang County's dead are sent there, so it attracts many flesh-eating vultures. The *tokden* there has only been doing the work for ten years, but has already helped over a hundred sixty people pass through. He was my apprentice. The head lama is Tenzin Delek Rinpoche.[1]

"Cutting people up for burial takes practice; it cannot be done in an arbitrary way," Rinchen continued, squatting on the ground beside me. With a knife, he made a few scratches on a blue-green stone. The scratches represented a twisted human body and looked very lifelike. "First you have to cut the back, then you have to cut twice along the ribs, then you have to turn the body over and cut twice along the stomach. It's not done exactly the same way for everyone. For example, it's different with big people. For men, you have to cut at an angle, like this. For women, you have to cut vertically, and for monks, you have to cut according to the type of robe . . . "

While Rinchen was talking, I was taking a lot of pictures. Suddenly he asked me to take a photograph of him lying on the grass with his eyes closed and his arms and legs twisted in different directions. "Everyone who is sent to the sky-burial site starts off looking something like this," he said. "I want to see what I will look like after I am brought here, after I am dead. Please don't forget," Rinchen said very seriously. "You must send me the photos." Of course I promised that I would.

Standing up and pointing to the mountains in the distance, he said, "A few days ago people were disputing over boundaries on the grassland and a person was killed. If you had arrived a few days earlier, you could have seen how I cut that person. A huge number of vultures were flying around."

Actually, I had seen a sky burial before. Or, to be more precise, I had seen what could be called a sky burial, but it wasn't for a human being. In 1998, I had gone with a TV production team from Taiwan to see Tsurphu Monastery,[2] located in Toelung Dechen County, near Lhasa. During our stay, we paid a special visit to the monastery's sky-burial site.

The production team wanted to film the burial process, but human corpses aren't sent to the site every day. They therefore bought a cow's leg to use as a substitute. One of the monks took off his coat and wrapped the limb so that it resembled a human torso. After they placed it on the site and surrounded it with stones, two monks began burning incense and spreading *tsampa* and barley grain on the ground. Facing the sacred mountain, the sky-burial master sat beside the "corpse," began playing a drum and horn, and recited the Buddhist scriptures that call vultures to the sky burial. At this point, large carnivorous birds began to circle high overhead. We could hear a deep, haunting sound that made us shiver. The monk explained that you could identify which birds were vultures by their white armpit feathers; the others were either eagles or large crows. He said that over a hundred vultures inhabited the holy mountain. Tantric Buddhism considers vultures to be the fiercest category of *dakinis* [embodiments of cosmic female energy], known as *shasa khandro:* breath-takers, flesh-eaters, blood-drinkers, and bone-chewers.

The winds picked up, and the Tsurphu River was rushing at great speed. High above, the slowly circling vultures looked graceful, calm, and gentle, yet somehow arrogant. The leading edges of their enormous wings appeared grey and white; the broad part of their wings, all the way to the tips, was black. As the birds descended in a spiral, maneuvering in the wind, their trailing wing feathers spread open, like huge scissors. I was overwhelmed by the beauty.

When the sky-burial master had thoroughly chopped up the meat with his knife and smashed the bones with rocks, the vultures, one by one, gradually landed on the ground nearby. They tucked their wings in and looked almost comical as they staggered forward on legs and feet that seemed too skinny to support their thick bodies. (Actually, they reminded me of the way Rinchen walks.) The master threw pieces of meat to them, but they were in no rush to eat. They encircled the meat, hunched over with their heads down, and hissed. The master began talking to them in a warm, gentle voice, as if the vultures were his friends. A monk explained to us that the sky-burial master was inviting the "boss" of the vultures to take the first bite. Until the boss ate, the rest of the vultures would stay back. The master knew nearly every vulture by name, according to the monk. Presently, a particularly ferocious-looking vulture slowly stepped out of the crowd of birds and started to eat. Immediately, the rest rushed in and pushed each other out of the way to get their share. I heard the sky-burial master saying, "Hey! Do not fight; there is enough for all of you."

More and more vultures landed, hissing and making their strange noises. I counted about eighty. "It is quite rare to see so many vultures," the sky-burial master told me excitedly. "Sometimes only a few come, even if a human corpse is here." When that happens, the sky-burial master explained, it is because the person had committed so many sins, the vultures considered the corpse too dirty to eat. When a lot of vultures show up and won't eat the corpse, it is because the family of the dead person failed to perform the religious funeral rites. Today was quite unique, a monk said, because they had asked His Holiness Karma Kuchen Rinpoche for special permission and instructions. This sky burial had thus received His Holiness's blessings and empowerment.

The sky-burial master, a former monk of Tsurphu Monastery, was over sixty years old. When I asked him about his occupation, he said that he was continually inspired by the story of Buddha compassionately feeding his own body to the hungry tiger. The master imagined he was each corpse as he chopped it up and fed it to the *shasa khandro dakinis* of the Ten Directions. In that way, he said, he believed his occupation was sacred.

What about Rinchen—how did he become a *tokden*? (Having gotten off-track with so many digressions, I am finally turning to this important question.) Rinchen told me, "Originally, I was a nomad, like all my ancestors on the Horra grasslands. I considered becoming a monk, but when 'democratic reforms' started, the Party working group tried to turn me into a revolutionary cadre. They saw, though, that I was too softhearted and couldn't help being concerned about the horses and cows whenever they got sick or injured. So, I became a veterinarian, because the Revolution also needed vets.

"One thing the Revolution did not need was *tokden*. For quite a long time, sky burials were banned here, since the practice was considered to be among the 'Four Olds' that the Cultural Revolution wanted to destroy.[3] As a result, the dead were either buried in the ground or secretly thrown into rivers. For the families of the deceased, nothing could have been worse: the souls of those who did not go through the sky-burial ceremony could not escape from purgatory, and most probably became ghosts. After the Cultural Revolution period ended, Tenzin Delek Rinpoche said to me, 'I noticed that you are very kind to the livestock; you even suck their wounds. This means you possess compassion for the dead as well and are highly suitable to be a *tokden*.' By this time, I had joined the Communist Party. It had never occurred to me that a Party member could become a *tokden*. But without a *tokden*, people were suffering an unsafe and uneasy death, which is a horrible thing. In addition, the most popular Communist Party slogan is 'Serve the People,' and to be a *tokden* is serving the people."

It was surprising to see how Rinchen had put Chairman Mao's guidance into practice. I praised him by saying, "Rinchen, across all of China—no, across the whole world—you are the only member of the Communist Party who is a *tokden*." And then I changed my tone and asked sternly, "Do you receive any payment?"

Rinchen flashed his snow-white teeth at me as if in ridicule, but actually with goodwill. By this time, we had reached the Horra township government building and dismounted. The setting sun had turned the mountains behind the sky-burial site a golden yellow. The beauty was stunning and incomparable. Rinchen went into his office and came back with a large sheet of white paper. He drew two columns on the paper, then began to fill them in with names followed by numbers. What did it mean?

Rinchen explained, "This is a list of all the dead persons for whom I performed sky burial. These are their names, and in this column are the amounts of money their families offered me. The families themselves decided the amounts: five *yuan,* ten *yuan,* twenty *yuan,* up to fifty *yuan.* It is fine with me if they do not have any money: I just put down a zero. But why have I drawn this list for you? It is because I want to show that I remember these people. I do not spend any of this money on myself. I have enough in salary, a little over two hundred *yuan.* I give some of these payments to the poor, and the rest goes to repairing places used for prayer."

I was very interested. Judging by the way he kept records, it was obvious that Rinchen was a responsible civil servant. A common nomad would have kept records by tying knots or using some other primitive method. I was deeply moved by the way Rinchen practiced his unique profession.

At that point, Tenzin called us in for dinner. He had stayed at the county government office to cook for us. I was pleasantly surprised that he had not only fried shredded potatoes, but also cooked mushrooms that he and Chodrak had found, mixing these with canned pork. The meal tasted very good.

Despite the peculiar smell that remained on his body, Rinchen had dinner with us. We were able to ignore it even though the room in the building was quite small. It was sparsely furnished, with a shaky table, four rickety wooden stools, and a steel stove for heating tea and cooking. Firewood was scattered all over the floor. Oh, yes; there was also an old, yellow, rotary-dial phone on the table. The space served as the government meeting room for the township. It couldn't be called just the township's office because it was also the meeting space for the Women's Federation, Youth League Committee, Office of Family Planning, and People's Armed Forces Division. However, nobody from these groups was around and all business was closed. As I mentioned earlier, all the civil servants had gone to look for mushrooms. Outside, some monks wearing robes were playing basketball. They were from the nearby monastery and had been asked to temporarily take care of the routine government matters. I noticed that they were carrying the keys to several offices, so I teased them by asking, "Isn't this the same as seizing power?"

Actually, there was one civil servant on duty. His name was Kelsang Gonpo. I cannot remember what his title was, but I still remember his unusual appearance and manner. He had messy curly hair, a dark complexion, and eyes as big as a yak's, which were red from drinking. Chodrak said harshly to him, when he entered the room, "You are a complete alcoholic!" Paying no attention, Kelsang Gonpo roughly dialed the rotary phone. Supposedly, dialing this phone would make all the telephones in the four nearby townships ring. But the switchboard was closed. To my amazement, he eventually managed to make this outdated communication device work, reaching a township leader who had just returned from looking for mushrooms. In his weird Chinese, Kelsang Gonpo shouted into the telephone, "Whether you come back soon or not, people are on the verge of being killed over here! Whether you come back or not, we have no power to settle their disagreements!" It turned out that the government recently had been redrawing the border between Nyakchuka and Lithang Counties, triggering territorial disputes among nomads from both counties. Apparently, over fifty nomads from Yonru, Lithang, had banded together and were determined to take back their traditional grasslands, which had been allocated to other people when the borders were redrawn. Dissatisfaction was also increasing among nomads in nearby places.

A heated discussion on the important subject of boundary settlements was soon underway in that small room. Disputes over grassland boundaries were never ending in the Tibetan nomadic areas. Almost every year, disputes among townships, counties, regions, and prefectures became so intense that lives were lost. The primary cause of the grassland disputes began in the 1950s, when Tibetan areas were divided into several new administrative regions. Now, after a series of failures, all levels of government had run out of ideas for dealing with the problem. Even if soldiers were dispatched, it made no difference. The only effective solutions came about when disputes were handled by a person highly respected by everyone, such as Tenzin Delek Rinpoche, who had settled conflicts a number of times. But let me stop my digression here and return to discussing Rinchen.

It started raining heavily, and rolling thunder boomed through the darkness. Lightning struck the telephone line hanging through the window, creating a burst of dazzling sparks. Screaming as though his hair had been set on fire, Kelsang Gonpo ran from the room. I lit candles that I had brought and continued listening to Rinchen's story. The lightning seemed to have ignited some deep, suppressed passion in him. His whole body became animated. Words and expressions in his native Nyuchangwa language came rushing out. The sound of Rinchen's Nyuchangwa overlapped with more thunder and the voices of Chodrak and Tenzin as they tried simultaneously to act as interpreters. All that's on my tape recorder is a jumble of noise, so I'm unable to retrieve Tokden Rinchen's wonderful expressions. It is a great shame. However, I did take down the following sentences:

> Life is short and uncertain. Today you see this person herding yaks; tomorrow he may be sent for sky burial. So I, too, do not know when I will be eaten by the vultures. Maybe I will still be here in ten years, or maybe I will die in a few days. Every time I cut a corpse, I think of myself as the dead person, and I pray that I will have a good reincarnation for the next life ... Whether diagnosing livestock or cutting a corpse, I was in the habit of eating *tsampa* without washing my hands, even though they were often covered in blood. I do not think of the blood as dirty. I believe the blood from other lives is the same as my own blood. One day, however, Tenzin Delek Rinpoche told me that while it was good that I cared for animals the same as I cared for human beings, it is not good to eat blood, which may carry viruses and affect my next life. Since then, I have abandoned my bad habit and now clean my hands before every meal.

Chodrak and Tenzin went outside to the toilet, and I was left alone listening to Rinchen, who continued speaking passionately. A sudden explosion of thunder and lightning blew out all the candles except one. In the dim, flickering light of the remaining candle, Rinchen's facial expressions changed constantly. They made me imagine all the dead people he had performed sky burial for. I became so terrified that I was about to run out when my two "bodyguards" came back.

The next day was sunny, without a trace of the heavy rain from the night before. The Horra grasslands were as beautiful as a lotus that has emerged from the water. Early in the morning, Rinchen came to say goodbye: four calves had died, and he had to go vaccinate the others. He held my hands for a long time. The peculiar smell still emanated from his body, but I was at ease with it. I now know why he was so kind and friendly to me. It is because I came from Lhasa, the holiest place for him. He gave me one hundred *yuan* and asked me to light butter lamps when I got back to Lhasa and to pray for the dead in front of Jokhang Temple. He said to me sadly—and it made me sad too—"If I am still alive in a few years, I will make a pilgrimage to Lhasa. I really want to go to the Jokhang Temple and see Jowo Rinpoche [Tibetan: Shakyamuni]."

As Rinchen mounted his horse and set off, I watched him gradually disappear into the distance. Although it could be said he had several identities, I understood that deep down he was, after all, a typical nomad. That identity had been given to him by history, but his identity seemed to me redundant now, and vanishing without a trace. It was futile to expect that I could have found in him the identity that I had sought in the beginning. Somehow, this made me feel sad, but also relieved. It is precisely the pluralism of their identities that turns a great many Tibetans into two, three persons, sometimes even more. What I mean is that I have seen many Tibetans with divided hearts and personalities. For instance, I know elderly people who have been given the identity "retired civil servant," and who lead meaningless lives with no sense of belonging. Of course, this is a complicated topic. Therefore, I can only say that on this seemingly unchanging—and yet seemingly ever-changing—Horra grassland, Rinchen is simply Rinchen.

Two years later, I returned to Nyakchuka, but I did not see Rinchen. Chodrak said he was still alive, but was no longer a *tokden*. A year after that, I went to Nyakchuka once again, and Chodrak invited me for dinner. Unexpectedly, there at the dining table sat Rinchen, smiling at me. He looked much older, and when he smiled, I saw he had lost many teeth. When he was not smiling, the depth of his eye sockets and the thinness of his face made his head look like a skull. I noticed the old smell was no longer on his body. With a look of great satisfaction, he told me that his lifelong wish had finally been fulfilled: he had been to Lhasa and seen Jowo Rinpoche. He then said that he had planned to visit me in Lhasa, but was unaware that the city was so big and crowded. He had stood in the monastery and shouted my name, but to no avail. He told me he had received the photographs I had taken of him, and sure enough, he looked exactly like the corpses waiting for sky burial.

(April 4, 2004, Beijing)

Translation by Dechen Pemba

NOTES

1. In April 2002, Tenzin Delek Rinpoche, a widely revered reincarnated lama, was arrested and tortured. Convicted by the Chinese government of "inciting splittism," he was sentenced to death. After international appeals on his behalf, in 2005 his sentence was commuted to life imprisonment. Protests calling for his release continue.

2. The main monastery of the Karma Kagyu lineage of Tibetan Buddhism.

3. Old Customs, Old Culture, Old Habits, and Old Ideas.

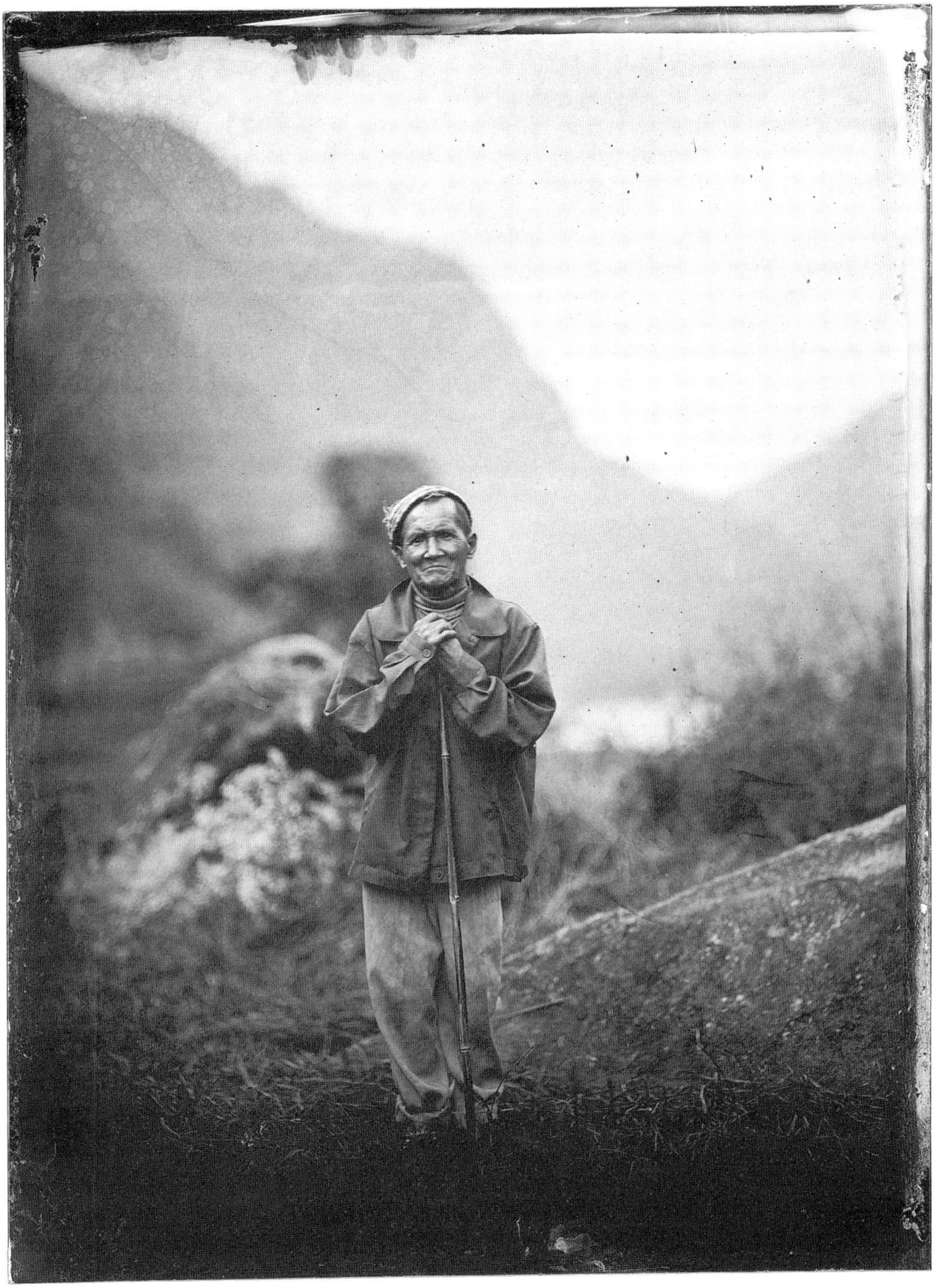

Luo Dan
Simple Song No. 23
Kai Axiang, Wawa Village
2010

蓝 蓝

四首诗

遗失

一个人遗失在信中。书中。
遗失在手离开后的灰尘里
以及椅子 灯光后
被用过的感情的轭具
以及列车呼啸而过的阴影——

他有着树叶和云彩的形状
在他的脚印里
有着积水映出的四季的形状

有时，某人会带着他 在
沉重发炎的膝关节里——
走向郊外 旧铁轨旁
在一丛被压倒的野蒿上
与另一个他相遇——

一个人遗失在被他遗失的
　　一切事物中。

消失

消失。
比死亡远，比拥抱近。
我接受遗产，你所奖赏的：
　　寂静。

你的旨意，我遵从。

在这横亘的安宁中我拥有
无限的时刻。广袤夜空中的群星。

LAN LAN

Four Poems

LOST

A man is lost in letters. In books.
Lost in the dust left by a hand
and chairs   after the lights
yokes of used feelings
and the shadow of a train whizzing past

He has the shape of leaves and clouds
In his footprints
the reflection of shapes of seasons

Sometimes, someone will accompany him   with
the seriously inflamed knee joints—
walking to the suburbs   near the old railways
above the defeated wild mugworts
to meet another him—

A man is lost in everything
        that he lost.

DISAPPEAR

Disappear.
Further than death, closer to a hug.
I accept legacy, what you award:
        silence.

Your decree, I obey.

In this transverse peace I own
instants of infinity. Stars in a vast night sky.

金色的你的身体在闪烁，到处都是。
金色的你的嘴唇。金色的！

麦田把它逝去的韶光种植在
我命运的屋顶。

大河村遗址

又一个大河村。
乌鸦在高高的杨树上静卧着
成群的麻雀飞过晒谷场
翅膀沾满金黄的麦芒
它们认出我。

微风还在几年前吹过
没有岁月之隔
我难道是另一个？

黄昏，长长的树影投向沙丘
又到了燃生炊火的时候
熟识的村民扛着铁锹
走在田埂上
牛驮着大捆的青草
像从前一样。我闪到一旁——

没有岁月之隔
只有大河村，这一动不动的
滔滔长河。

未完成的途中

……午夜。一行字呼啸着
冲出黑暗的隧道。幽蓝的信号灯
闪过。一列拖着脐带的火车
穿越桥梁，枕木下
我凹陷的前胸不断震颤。它紧抵
俯身降落的天空，碾平，伸展
——你知道，我

总是这样，摇晃着
在深夜起身，喝口水
坐下。信。电话线中嗡嗡的雪原。躺在
键盘上被自己的双手运走。翻山越岭

Your golden body is glittering, everywhere.
Your golden lips. Golden!

Wheat field plants its past glories
on the roof of my fate.

RUINS OF THE GREAT RIVER VILLAGE

Again a great river village.
Crows rest on tall poplars
sparrows fly over a grain-sunning ground
their wings tinted with a golden wheat shine
They recognize me.

Some years ago a breeze still blew
Timeless partition
Am I a partition?

At dusk, long tree shadows throw themselves to the dunes
Again time to raise a cooking fire
Familiar villagers carry shovels and spades
and walk in the fields
Oxen bear big bundles of grass
like before. I dodge—

a timeless partition
only the great river village, this still and
torrential flow of water.

UNFINISHED VOYAGE

. . . Midnight. A line of words howls,
dashing from a dark tunnel. A blue signal lamp
flashes. Train, hauling cars by an umbilical cord,
crosses the bridge. Under the sleepers
my chest can't stop shaking. It resists
the bent falling sky, flattens, and expands
—You know, I

am always this way, wavering,
getting up late at night, drinking water,
sitting down. Mail. Snow fields hum in the phone line. On
the keyboard my hands travel over mountains and valleys.

从水杉的尖顶上沉沉扫过，枝条
划破饥渴的脸。或者，贴着地面
冰碴挂上眉毛，你知道，有时

我走在纬四路的楝树下，提着青菜
推门，仿佛看到你的背影，孩子们快乐尖叫
冲过来抱着我的腿。雨从玻璃上滴落。
屋子晃动起来，轮子无声地滑行
拖着傍晚的炊烟。那时，市声压低了

楼下的钉鞋匠，取出含在嘴里的钉子
抡起铁锤，狠狠地楔进生活的鞋底，毫不
犹豫。这些拾荒的人
拉着破烂的架子车，藏起捡到的分币
粗大的骨节从未被摧毁。你知道，端午时节

蒿草浓烈的香气中，我们停靠的地方
布谷鸟从深夜一直叫到天亮，在远处的林子里
躲在树荫下面。你睫毛长长的眼睛
闭着。手边是放凉的水杯和灰烬的余烟。站在窗前，
我想：我爱这个世界。在那
裂开的缝隙里，我有过机会。
它缓缓驶来，拐了弯……

我总是这样。盯着荧屏，长久地
一行字跳出黑暗。黝黝的田野。矿灯飞快地向后
丘陵。水塘。夜晚从我的四肢碾过。
凄凉。单调。永不绝望
你知道，此时我低垂的额头亮起
一颗星：端着米钵。摇动铁轮的手臂
被活塞催起——火苗窜上来。一扇窗口
飘着晾晒的婴儿尿布，慢慢升高了……

As I sweep past the tops of redwoods, branches
scratch my hungry face, or perhaps, close to the ground
ice crystals emerge and hang on my eyebrows. You know, sometimes

I walk under japonicas along Weisi Road, carrying vegetables,
pushing open the door. I seem to see you from behind, children
shriek happily
rushing to hug my legs. Rain drips from the windowpane.
The house shakes, wheels glide past without a sound,
hauling evening kitchen smoke. City noise falls.

Downstairs, a cobbler takes a nail from his mouth
and wields a hammer, driving it violently into the sole of life, without
hesitation. These rag-and-bone men
pull broken carts, hide any coins they find,
their thick joints barely worn out. You know, at Dragon Boat Festival

in thick fragrance of wormwood, we stop where
cuckoos call from night till daybreak, lying in the shade
in a distant forest. Your long eyelashes
close. A cup turning cold at hand and the last smoke from ashes.
Before the window,
I'm thinking: *I love this world.* There,
a fissure opens, my chance is here.
It turns toward me slowly, around the curve . . .

I am always this way. Staring forever at the screen.
A line of words jumps out of the dark. Black fields. A miner's lamp
flies backward.
Hills. Ponds. Night runs over my limbs.
Desolation. Monotony. Never despair.
You know, at this instant, my head lowered, a star shines
on my brow. I carry a rice bowl. Arms moving iron wheels
are driven by the piston—flames gush forth. By a window
drying diapers flutter, and slowly rise . . .

Translations by Fiona Sze-Lorrain

三首詩

寫詩是可恥的

奧茨維辛之後，寫詩是可恥的。
八八風災之後，寫詩是可恥的。
只要還有人餓肚子，寫詩是可恥的。
跟家人借錢不還的人，寫詩是可恥的。
剛剛壓死了兩隻螞蟻的人，寫詩是可恥的。
連字都寫不好的人，寫詩是可恥的。
不夠孤獨的人，寫詩是可恥的。
一再的確認了各種羞恥之後，還要寫詩。
我是可恥的。
不管怎樣，我要寫詩。
一再的確認，我要寫詩……

除了寫詩的羞恥，我不願忍受其他的羞恥。

2010

生 ／日

這一天，我聽到某種召喚
那絕非來自光明

這一天，我感受到喪子之痛
但我卻沒有兒女
我失去所愛
卻不知我愛的是什麼

這一天，我只想大睡一場
從另一個夢中醒來
丟掉必須穿衣的禮貌

YINNI

Three Poems

IT IS SHAMEFUL TO WRITE POETRY

after Auschwitz, it is shameful to write poetry
after the August 8th flood, it is shameful to write poetry
as long as there's someone starving, it is shameful to write poetry
for someone who doesn't pay back a debt, it is shameful to write
  poetry
for someone who has crushed two ants, it is shameful to write poetry
for someone who can't write characters well, it is shameful to write
  poetry
for someone who is not lonely enough, it is shameful to write poetry
having acknowledged all forms of shame, yet still to be writing poetry
I am shameful
nothing matters, I continue to write poetry
acknowledging this fact again and again, I continue to write poetry . . .

I refuse to suffer all shame except the shame of writing poetry

(2010)

BIRTH-DAY

on this day, I heard a calling
but it didn't come from any light

on this day, I feel the pain of losing my son
but I have no children
I have lost my beloved
but I don't know who I loved

on this day, all I want to do is get a long sleep
wake up from another dream
forget the etiquette of covering myself with clothes

胡思亂想的惡習
露出尖牙與利齒

這一天，我想要記住
活著就是一種恥辱
我的美德與笑容
都已耗盡

這一天，我想要知道
什麼樣的人
該受什麼樣的苦？
什麼樣的夢
才會是最後一個夢？

2009

足夠的死

沒有一個死者能帶走什麼
沒有一個死者不留下什麼

未完成的計畫
未獲回覆的信
來不及銷毀的作品
垃圾、八卦、負債、襪子上的黴菌……

在死後仍持續增加的敵人與朋友
在死後仍持續成長的一張臉
終將代替了，原來的臉

沒有一個死亡，足夠消滅
沒有一個地獄，足夠遙遠

2010

bad habits of fantasizing
and showing my menacing sharp teeth

on this day, I'd like to remember
to live is to live in shame
all my virtues and smiles
have been depleted

on this day, I'd like to know
what kind of person
deserves what kind of suffering?
what kind of dream
is the last dream?

(2009)

ENOUGH DEATH

not a single person can die and take something with him
not a single person dies without leaving something behind

projects to be completed
letters to reply to
writings to be burned
trash, gossip, debts, mold on one's socks . . .

after a person dies, enemies and friends continue to multiply
after a person dies, his face continues to grow
till in the end it overtakes the original face

not a single death is enough to destroy it all
not a single hell is far enough

(2010)

Translations by Michelle Yeh

宇 向

八首诗

理所当然

当我年事已高　有些人
依然会　千里迢迢
赶来爱我　而另一些人
会再次抛弃我

8月17日天气预报

各位观众，大家好！
现在向您播报今夜和
明天的天气状况：
23点至凌晨3点左右
两条在黑暗中
交媾的蛇将降临泺源大街，
它们经常尾随刺客入室
请该街的住户关好门窗，
同时《幻想即兴》会随风起舞，
并伴有W形闪电。
请大家上网时注意东经40，
北纬117.9的逆向时速，
一定避开后现代女权思潮。
另外，明晨气温将继续下降，
处女膜修补术、
男性生殖器二次发育液
将同西伯利亚寒流一起
从报纸中缝向偏南方向移动，
并在泉城广场上空停留，
短时有流星雨，
提醒大家注意防范爱情，
不然幸福会令你吃尽苦头。
今天的天气预报播送完了，
谢谢收看。

Y U   X I A N G

Eight Poems

IT GOES WITHOUT SAYING

when I'm old some
will still travel miles
to love me but others
will once again jilt me

WEATHER FORECAST, AUGUST 17

ladies and gentlemen, hello!
here is the weather forecast for tonight
and tomorrow
from 2300 till 3 in the morning
two snakes copulating in the dark
will arrive at Luoyuan Street
they often trail assassins into the house
residents, please shut your doors and windows
the "Fantasie Impromptu" will begin its dance in the wind
accompanied by zigzag lightning
internet surfers, look out for a backward velocity
at longitude 40° east and latitude 117.9° north
and avoid postmodern feminist waves
temperatures will also continue to fall tomorrow morning
hymenoplasty
penis enhancement gel
and a cold front from Siberia
will creep southward along the central folds of a newspaper
and linger over the Fountain City Square
expect brief meteor showers
brace against love
if not, happiness will make you suffer
that's all for today's weather forecast
thank you for tuning in

绘画生涯

一

我得下决心去画一些户外景色。
就像每天上班，
必须经过那些臃肿的草莓和鸡，
经过禁书、性病、传说、
唱“回家看看”的乞丐夫妻、
篡改的历史、尘土或尾气般的
流窜犯，经过那些被一次一次挖开、
填平，结果再也添不平的
文化路、和平路、即时语录、
无端的愤怒……

二

我要去画表情和姿态，
在经期也不能停止，
以免警笛干扰笔尖的弯度和走向。
无论律法和公正如何背道而弛，
美女仍是一个活生生的奇迹，
她让生活像颜料一样消耗殆尽。
我的好同志，
只要我能在记忆中将你画出来，
那么我就永远有事可做

三

我要画一些静物，
廉价卖掉，用以糊口。
我从墙上取下前辈的奖牌和勋章，
上面布满辉煌的锈迹，
从箱底翻出一摞红皮证书，
再将客厅的指路明灯拧下，
为了抒情，我一遍一遍摆放它们，
这些没落贵族般的静物

四

没有光线，没有光线，
色彩像睡眠里的对话。
夜里，我直接将黑与白挤到画布上。

A PAINTING LIFE

1

I must make up my mind to paint some outdoor scenes
like going to work every day
must pass by those puffy strawberries and chickens
pass by illegal books, sex diseases, legends
a beggar couple singing "Visit Home"
a distorted history, a dusty
fugitive, like refinery tailings, dug and re-dug
filled but never finally leveled
Cultural Street, Peace Street, improvised quotes
and undefined anger . . .

2

I want to paint expression and posture
not even stopping when menstruating
lest sirens interfere with the brush's angle and direction
However law and justice may oppose
a beauty is still a living miracle
she spends away life like colors
My good comrade
as long as I can draw you in memory
I'll always have something to do

3

I want to paint some still lifes
sell them cheap to get by
I take down my forefathers' awards and medals
stained with glorious corrosion
dig out a pile of red leather diplomas from the bottom of a box
then unscrew the beacon lights in the living room
For a lyrical feel, I arrange them again and again
these still lifes, like the last nobles

4

No light, no light
colors, like a sleep dialogue
At night, I squeeze black and white right onto the canvas

白，涂抹鲜血，
黑，爆炸，
中间的灰调子近似于抽象的政府

五

有时，我画赤裸裸的声音。
当新闻联播里传出风声，
我仍听到双人床上的叫卖，
并在《阿姆斯特丹的河流》里
瞬间认出——“大海的巨大徘徊”
有人说：绘画使人堕落。
我就继续堕落

六

如果我还有力气，还有力气，
我会寄一幅给你。画面上
没有标题也没有签名，
像一个又一个流亡者

像人一样

很多东西在黑暗中像人一样
像那些坐着的站着的趴着的蹲着的蜷着的起伏的正在行走的
摆出各种姿势的人一样

在黑暗中所有的东西都像人，像人一样

像人一样惊吓你

比如树木座钟马桶扫帚空椅子有缺口的墙和石头
还有虚掩的窗户一大堆书一滩血迹或尿迹
以及一个或两个呆在黑暗里的人

女巫师

我高龄。能做任何人的祖母
当我右手举起面具
左手握住心，我必定

white smudges blood
black explodes
the gray in-between like an abstract government

5

Sometimes I paint nude voices
When a news broadcast brings the voice of wind,
from a double bed I can hear a street vendor
and in *River Amsterdam*
recognize instantly "the vast lingering of sea"
Someone says, *Drawing degenerates man*
I'll keep degenerating

6

If I still have the strength, still have the strength
I'll send you a painting, with
no title or signature
like one exile after another

LIKE HUMANS

many things in the dark are like humans
like those sitting standing lying squatting coiling rolling now walking
like humans in every pose

in the dark all things are human-like, like humans

startling you like humans do

such as trees desk clock toilet bowl broom empty chair chipped wall
    and stone
and an unlocked window a big pile of books a pool of blood or a
    urine stain
and one or two humans staying in the dark

SORCERESS

I reach a lofty age. Can be a grandmother to anyone
When my right hand lifts a mask
the left holds a heart. I'm indeed

货真价实。拥有古老的手艺
给老鼠剃毛。把烛台弄炸
被豹子吞噬。使马路柔肠寸断
分崩离析那些已分崩离析的人
我懂得羞涩的仪式
会忍痛割爱。当太阳自山头升起
照耀舞台中央的时候
我就是传统，无人逾越
当我把祭器高举
里面溅出幽灵的血。是我
在人间忍受着羞辱
我是思想界最大的智慧
最小的聪明。调换左右眼
就隐藏了慈悲和邪恶
而在每一个精确的时刻
我到纺织机后配制泪水
把换来的钱攒起来
现在我打算退休
成为平凡无害的人

窗

我想到的窗子是美丽的
因为它们框住了流动的风景
从里面看总是这样
我不知道外面的人怎样看
也不想知道
我妈妈的窗子在二十层
每次看到它
我都会有冲出去的想法
我自己的窗子在一层
它框住随意经过的人
和一个刻意到这里的人
我的办公室在地下
窗子开在最上方
在一个扁小的长方形里
我要抬头
才能看到污水、彷徨和失落

authentic, with ancient craftsmanship
to shave fur off mice. Or explode candlesticks
Devoured by leopards. I break roads
disintegrate people already disintegrated
I understand shy rituals
can bear to part with what I love. As the sun rises
lighting up the center stage
I'm the tradition, beaten by no one
As I uphold ritual vessels
ghost blood splatters. I'm the one
who bears humiliation in this world
In the realm of thoughts I'm the greatest wisdom
the pettiest wits. Switch both eyes
to hide mercy and evil
At each exact instant
I'll install tears behind spinning machines
accumulate the money in return
Now I plan to retire
as a harmless everyman

WINDOW

the windows I think of are beautiful
because they frame the shifting scenery
it always looks this way from the inside
I don't know how outsiders look
and don't want to know
my mother's window is on the twentieth floor
each time I see it
I'll think of dashing out
my own window is on the first floor
it frames casual passersby
and a specific guest
my office is underground
the window opens right above
in a small and narrow rectangle
I must look up
to see sewage, hesitation and dejection

苍蝇狂想曲

走进饭店后院
一阵黑冰雹
密集地砸过来

又硬又亮的盾牌肚皮
黄水晶圆玛瑙的头
人还没有反应过来
有一些已经弹了出去
落在毛皮残缺的一堆断羊腿上
那是猎人用扭曲生锈的铁丝网
罩住猎物

另一些又粘了一会
在人的袖口　衣领　脖子　脸　眼睛　周围
用细长的腿或者舌头
（已经分不清是腿还是舌头）
有几个钻进头发里
以为找到了它们的黑丛林

你驱赶，它们就更多更凶猛
碰撞　纠缠　紧逼　不顾一切
呻吟
这是高原上的声音
这是最野蛮的爱：
——敌对，亲吻

渡夜

新年一过，我们就步行

县西巷，营业中的酒馆
灯箱是去年的光
爆竹震响电话
有人在我们身上互拜晚年
哈气，在椅背上蹭出油渍和焰火

酒馆里，从不缺少孤独的人

不缺少疲倦的交谈
渡夜的人
在稚气和病态间摇摆

FANTASIA OF A HOUSEFLY

walking into the hotel's backyard
black hailstones
came pounding down in clusters

hard and shiny belly shields
round citrine agate heads
humans had yet to react
some had already sprung out
landing on a mutilated pile of severed lamb legs
those were twisted rusty barbed wires hunters used
to entrap prey

others stuck themselves again
around humans' cuffs collars necks faces eyes
with fine, long legs or tongues
(legs or tongues already indiscernible)
a few made their way into hair
thinking they had found their black forests

you drove them away, they multiplied and turned more savage
colliding entangling pressing recklessly
moaning
this is the voice in the highlands
this is the most barbaric love
—oppose, kiss

CROSSING NIGHT

once New Year is over, we shall walk

Xianxi Lane, pubs in business
light boxes are lights from last year
firecrackers deafen phones
someone exchanges belated new year wishes over us
exhale, to smear grease and fireworks on the backs of chairs

pubs never lack lonely men

never lack weary conversations
men crossing night
sway between childishness and sallowness

要糟蹋些什么，活着
要亵渎些什么
冬天仍在啤酒里
两块冰块彼此稀释
明天，他们仍然
要与一些继续生活的人交错而过

仍然要步行
要记忆里重逢着被捏碎的容颜
我们，一眼认出那个背叛的人

to ruin so-and-so, live
to profane so-and-so
winter is still in the beer
two pieces of ice dilute each other
tomorrow, they still
must cross paths with some who continue life

still must walk
must reunite in memory with crumbled faces
we recognize that traitor at first sight

Translations by Fiona Sze-Lorrain

孙 磊

四首诗

我的歌厅生意

我得雇一些女人
在她们额上掀动黄昏，

给她们线，不给线头。
疼她们，不怜悯。

我多么熟悉她们身上的豹子，
热血让树叶哗哗作响。

在她们的喘息里
我得说到瓷，深渊，

但我恨我的冷漠
在她们身上变为寂静。

我得学得像她们一样
点钱，唱跑调的歌，爱不值得爱的人……

我得雇她们教我
去没有野心地绝望地生活。

我往前走了几步

我往前走了几步，
街面宽阔、冰冷，像削平的铁板。
人像火烧着，狠狠地，彼此，越来越多
淤积在偶尔的抽泣、踌躇和盲目中。

SUN LEI

Four Poems

MY NIGHTCLUB BUSINESS

I must hire some women
stir dusk on their foreheads

give them thread, not thread ends
adore them, not pity them

I know so well the leopards on their bodies
hot blood that shuffles leaves

In their panting
I must evoke porcelain, abyss

But I hate my aloofness
that turns into stillness on their bodies

I must learn to be like them
count money, sing off-key, love those who are unworthy of love . . .

I must hire them to teach me
to live without ambition and despondently

I ADVANCE A FEW STEPS

I advance a few steps.
Wide, icy street, like a dressed iron plate.
People burn one another, like fire, cruelly, increasingly
silted up in sporadic sobs, hesitation and aimlessness.

故乡 2002

冬天。一个巨大国度的遗容在我手上是枝条也是镣铐。
白日正落向我充满石灰的荫沉但缠绕杂声的身体。

不是结尾，是纪念

突然收住，
黑暗在缰绳手里，
有一条告别之路。

一小匙糖在风中，
衣领在甲板上，
祖国在剁肉的案板里
碎成一个家。

哭泣倒下，
我不需要任何人，
为我站着。

把一条街站斜，
把死亡
站成一排排僵直的
广场之树。

HOMELAND 2002

Winter. Remains of a colossal country are branches as well as
handcuffs in my hands.
Daylight is falling on my body shrouded in decayed lime but twined
in a cacophony.

NOT THE END, BUT A MEMORIAL

Abruptly withdrawn
darkness in the hands of reins
has a farewell road

A teaspoon of sugar in the wind
shirt collar on a deck
Motherland shatters into a family
on a chopping board

Weeping falls
I need no one
to stand for me

Stand till a street tilts
Stand up death
in rows of stiff trees
in the square

Translations by Fiona Sze-Lorrain

朵 渔

四首诗

聚集

冬雨聚集起全部的泪
湿漉漉的落叶犹如黑色的纸钱

一个男人在上坡，他竖起的肩膀
聚集起全部的隐忍

松针间的鸟，聚集起全部的灰
雨丝如飘发，聚集成一张美丽的脸

我站在窗前，看那玻璃上的水滴
聚集成悲伤的海

什么样的悲伤会聚集成力
取决于你的爱

一颗子弹在天上飞

一颗子弹在天上飞
一颗铜质子弹，反射着太阳的光芒
在天上飞
像静止一样，那样迅疾
在芝诺的直线上
飞
是什么样的基础、什么样的情仇
什么样的抛物线
将它送上了天
一颗子弹
一刻不停地
在天上飞

DUO YU

Four Poems

GATHERING

Winter rain gathers all the tears
Moist fallen leaves, black like burnt ghost money

A man uphill, with shoulders raised
gathers all endurance

Birds between pine needles gather all the ashes
Threads of rain floating like hair, gather into a beautiful face

I stand by the window, looking at drops of water on the pane
gather into a sea of sorrow

What sorrow can gather into a force
It depends on your love

A BULLET FLIES IN THE SKY

a bullet flies in the sky
a copper-jacketed bullet, reflecting the radiant sun
flies in the sky
like in stillness, so speedy
flying
over Zeno's straight lines
what base, what revenge
what parabola
will send it into the sky
a bullet
ceaselessly
flies in the sky

抬头张望的人
张大了嘴巴
无人知晓
这颗子弹
它到底
意欲何为
它在飞。

玻璃上的雨

一阵小风之后
窗帘微微吹起

雨落在屋瓦上
雨落在自行车上
雨落在夜里

那滞留于玻璃上的雨滴
像一群飞蛾
被台灯照亮

我看见孤魂一闪
一张美丽的脸
她在我身后
仿佛已多年

雨季开始了

最后的黑暗

走了这么久
我们是该坐在黑暗里
好好谈谈了
那亮着灯光的地方
就是神的村落，但要抵达那里
还要穿过一片林地
你愿意跟我一起
穿过这最后的黑暗吗？
仅仅愿意
还不够，因为时代的野猪林里

people staring with heads up
open their mouths wide
no one knows
what exactly
this bullet
desires when
it flies

RAIN ON GLASS PANE

after a light wind
curtains stir

rain falls on tiles
rain falls on bicycles
rain falls in the night

raindrops linger on the glass pane
like a whisper of moths
lit by a desk lamp

I see a lonely ghost in a flash
a beautiful face
she is behind me
as if for many years

the season of rain has begun

THE LAST DARKNESS

after walking for so long
we should sit down in the dark
and have a good talk
the place lit by a lamp
is the village of God, but to reach there
still a forest to go through
are you willing to come with me
through this last darkness
simply being willing
isn't enough—in this era the wild land of boars*

* *Location in the novel* The Water Margin, *where the hero Lin Chong is nearly assassinated*

布满了光明的暗哨和猎手
你要时刻准备着
把我的尸体运出去
光明爱上灯
火星爱上死灰
只有伟大的爱情
才会爱上灾难。

is full of open surveillance and hunters
you must be ready anytime
to carry my corpse out
light loves lamp
sparks love dead ashes
only great love
can love disasters

Translations by Fiona Sze-Lorrain

KAREN AN-HWEI LEE

Vestiges of Sea Pilgrims

Water on Sunset Boulevard

On Los Angeles's 230th anniversary, Emily Dickinson and I cruise the city.

Vernal greenery. We stay on Sunset in search of water. Two unlikely sisters, Emily and I are a pair of cool Berkshire fronds this afternoon. Atlantic sea pilgrims. Woodland ferns. I grew up in Massachusetts before moving to greater Los Angeles. Emily, who lived in the Berkshires her entire life, is no longer alive. Fiddleheads and orchid kin. Lady slippers. No shops, no boutiques, no dermatologists, no glass edifices. Ornamental shade only, trees never sacrificed for poles or coffins. I talk while driving even if no one's there. To live at the end of a blind driveway, I say. You mean an unseen one, Emily says. We drive on Sunset, rows of trees: cedars, stands of white pine, evergreens, junipers twisted in funnel clouds. Blindness. Trees conceal the houses, glimpsed now and then.

Our childhood in Massachusetts, I say.
Trees, trees, murmurs Emily.

The boulevard curves past a cast-iron Bel-Air gate, no signs except citadels of trees. Basilicas of air. Groves of sky. I lived here as a girl, says Emily. Sunset is a myth, I say. No one lives this way, among sentinel firs in Los Angeles. It costs multi-millions to do this. It's the location, I say. Location is in the heart, says Emily. In the cathedral of a soul. One underground river sustains greenery by night, originating from a glacier lake in Beverly Hills. Jurassic glaciers, underground caverns of Los Angeles.

There aren't any of those here, I say.
Where are glacier hills, says Emily.
None, I say. You're thinking of Burbank.

La Brea Tar Pits, she coughs. Brea tar flows on the Orange Freeway, black as the spice cake in the basket I once lowered into my garden.

Silence.

Were the Berkshires formed by glaciers?

Water on Rodeo Drive

Did you ever grow heather, Emily?

Silence.

Radishes?

Emily shakes her head. I only remember the daylilies.

We're lost, Emily and I. We choose a road with a whimsical name, Rodeo. Of course, Rodeo Drive, the famous one. Shops and boutiques with silk gloves but no ambient music. Strangers photograph one another on a cobbled alley with a steep grade. Los Angelenos, who live in the city year round, do not. Take photographs. Almost vertical: a movie set? Is it Boston, where Emily visited her eye doctor? High noon, yet flash bulbs spark magnesium in the sun. Venice, I say. No, Vegas, Emily says, adjusting her snood, auburn hair awry. Venice section of Vegas, she explains. *Venezia.* I can tell by walking on it. The stones are machine eroded, not foot worn. You tell genuine sea glass this way, too.

We visit an Italian zapateria to ask about women's shoes.

Zapateria is Spanish, I say.

Are you sure this isn't Paris? says a tourist.

We're sure this isn't Paris, we say.

Emily, can you speak another language? I ask, but she does not reply. Odor is a saloon in a desert. Saloon, echoes Emily, as an afterthought. It's not a word I used often when I was alive. A saleswoman, two salesmen, and a third man who doesn't identify himself, a fashion spy, emerge from leather-clad halls to hear a tale I recount with raised hands, my ancient mariner toast to wedding guests: *Listen! Once upon a time, a woman grew large bone spurs, also called onions, eleven and a half wide . . .* We hear tongues in Russian, Portuguese, Czech, Vietnamese. Everyone comes to Rodeo Drive.

Bunions, says Emily.

Not onions?

I remember narcissus.

Not the daylilies?

A flash bulb strikes. Not white magnesium, we remind ourselves. Not stars. White chrysanthemums. On a street corner, an evangelist shares the gospel in Japanese: イエス・キリスト. We listen closely. Parking meters hum tangible minutes in a digital staccato. Emily says the parking meters remind her of grave mounds and tombstones in the Berkshires. A person is looking at you, she comments, but it is not a person. The hum summons her memories of the sea.

Salt, says Emily. Rime.
I thought you never saw the sea.
I must have. I know what a wave is.

Water on Wilshire Boulevard

Boutiques are closed although it's ten forty-five in the morning. It's too early, I say, opening a lacquered bento box for me and Emily. Everyone is sleeping. Los Angeles is nocturnal. The shops open at eleven unless caffeine is sold; then they open at ten. Emily abstains from coffee. Her kidneys are weak; they killed her. Bright's disease. Drink lots of water, says Emily. We love to touch water fountains. Bronze wells, crystal pillars, engraved brass, wings. We're thirsty pilgrims. None we wish to buy is sold here. We eat the California rolls I've packed for lunch and stroll past a jewelry store selling enormous pearls, an invisible ocean of oysters nowhere seen, yet secreting gems—black, gold, pale coral—in a manhole under the sidewalk. See the nacreous evidence in the boutiques. Blue hyacinth, lavender. Hydrangea. The water is nonpotable, but we are grateful for salt and light from a beach miles away in Venice.

Venice Beach is not Venice in Italy, she says.
I mean Los Angeles County, where we are now.
Venezia.

Water in La Cienega Heights

We walk under a freeway overpass.
A ghetto, or this is *ghetto,* not a ghetto.

Who is the Baal Shem Tov? asks Emily, studying the freeway art.
A mystic Jewish rabbi, I say.

Was he alive when I was alive?
No, I don't think either of us was born yet.

Emily wants a tattoo of a dove, a sea wave.
Why?

My letter, she whispers: to the world.

Water in East Los Angeles

Where are the angels, we say in a glass-strewn lot, on a sidewalk Emily says is littered with rope-weeds, in front of a television station rising in the sun, obsidian dome without windows. Noon, seventy-two degrees, unusually cool for summer, yet asphalt retains heat in shadow. Emily has never seen asphalt before. She kneels down in her white dress. Asphalt looks like black spice cake after sitting in the cellar for two weeks. I say it is midnight, a hot silk cloak of Santa Ana winds. Or no wind. We seek water. Vestiges of sea pilgrims. We ask to use a restroom in the television station. Is there anyone in the building who can sign you in, the receptionist intones. It is not a question.

A glass bowl, paper hydrangeas.
You can sign us in, we say.
The woman says: I don't know you.

So we walk to the newspaper headquarters, where we explain without riddles or rhymes: We are tired, lost, and thirsty. We seek an oasis. You poor sisters, says the receptionist, pointing to the elevator, assuming we are nuns in habit who seek a women's restroom. Emily is wearing a brown fustian, not her favorite white dress: I don't wear my pajamas or my house dress for travel, she says, even after death.

Up one floor, take a right. As we turn, she watches us on blue-flickering security cameras.

Angels unawares, we say. Traveling mercies, grace for strangers.
How far is the Pacific Coast Highway?

Water in West Hollywood

Yes. We walk around in the dog park, where Emily says, Let's go. She loves children and animals but feels nervous around large dogs. We walk around the corner to Santa Monica Boulevard. Men walk muscular dogs. Jowls and haunches squat on ruined sidewalks. No one says anything. Order a carriage to take us, says Emily, yet death is in the carriage. A young man with strong features—aquiline nose—sweeps the gutter tenderly, as though drying chrysanthemums for tea. We pass a sushi bistro which isn't a sushi bistro. It only opens at night, one windowpane cracked in fifteen parts. The door is above a sill, no knob on the outside. Maybe the owner drops a rope ladder at night. Maybe the chefs bleed fresh sashimi on the premises during the day.

We receive directions to a museum from a man at a construction site. This is for a museum of dismembered parts, says the man. Prosthetics, I say. Parsons, says Emily. He says: No, dismembered parts. We do not ask questions. After walking through a gulley of broken glass, we arrive at the small museum, knock on the maroon-slatted door, and enter into darkness. We are informed the museum is free. A woman on film shrieks *Fire fire* in the first exhibit. Emily believes the woman is shrieking in the language of Furies, but it's English. Emily, do you know Latin or Greek? I ask. Emily does not reply. How do you know the Furies? I ask Emily. Silence. Then Emily says, The question is: How would *you* know? The camera pans over a kitchen, broken dishes, ashtrays. Chairs without arms, and arms without chairs. We go into the elevator. Emily's face blanches. The elevator thumps like a garbage bin on the way up. The door opens. A cinema screen with dismembered furniture, arms, legs. Ah, says Emily. I was afraid my cherry-wood writing desk ended up as firewood. The elevator door closes.

A voice says into cinematic darkness: Feel as though I've seen this film nine times.

Your furniture wasn't chopped up for firewood, Emily. It's in a museum.

What about the little desk by the window, the chairs, my bed at the Homestead?

Those are cherry-wood replicas, Emily. Your white dress was copied thousands of times.

Her sherry eyes widen. This isn't my dress?

No, the dress you're wearing is yours.

We wash our hands in the restroom, which is mirrored, well lit, and clean. Outside, the streets are adult. The streets are furious. Vans and ravens. A raven-man on a bicycle arrives at the museum and peeps inside. His ravenous eyes alight on us. We open the maroon door, now blood hued, to escape. Emily has never seen a horror film before, only dreamed them. Do we still use the word *nightmare?* asks Emily. Yes. Streets run across sidewalks through the vestibule littered with broken glass and into the utility poles where ravens roost.

Not an angel, although Emily says it's possible, you never know.

We are not on a search for angels, I remind Emily.

Why is it called the City of Angels?

Water on Figueroa

We take a detour to the 110 South, but original signs for the freeway remain. Some signs are upside-down. Others are detour signs, right-side up. We cannot tell which is which. We circle downtown for an hour before asking for directions. I ask at a station where the gas price is astronomical, as it is everywhere in Los Angeles.

Go straight on this avenue until Figueroa, then turn right.

I go straight and turn right on Figueroa, but the signs say 110 South, U-turn. They also say: 110 South, Figueroa, pointing the way I came, not Figueroa. Either the man at the gas station actually meant stage left and stage right—not ordinary left and right—or the signs are infinite mirrors. Getting lost is an opportunity to go sightseeing. On 8th Street, we spot a new sign: 110 South, 110 North. The street is one-way to the left. I am in the wrong lane: the right one. No different from driving in Boston, I say, without the tunnels or Big Dig.

In a mirage, I see whales breaching in the harbor.
I haven't been out of the house in years, says Emily.
How does it feel? I ask.
A good thing you're driving.
Why?
I never drove in Amherst.

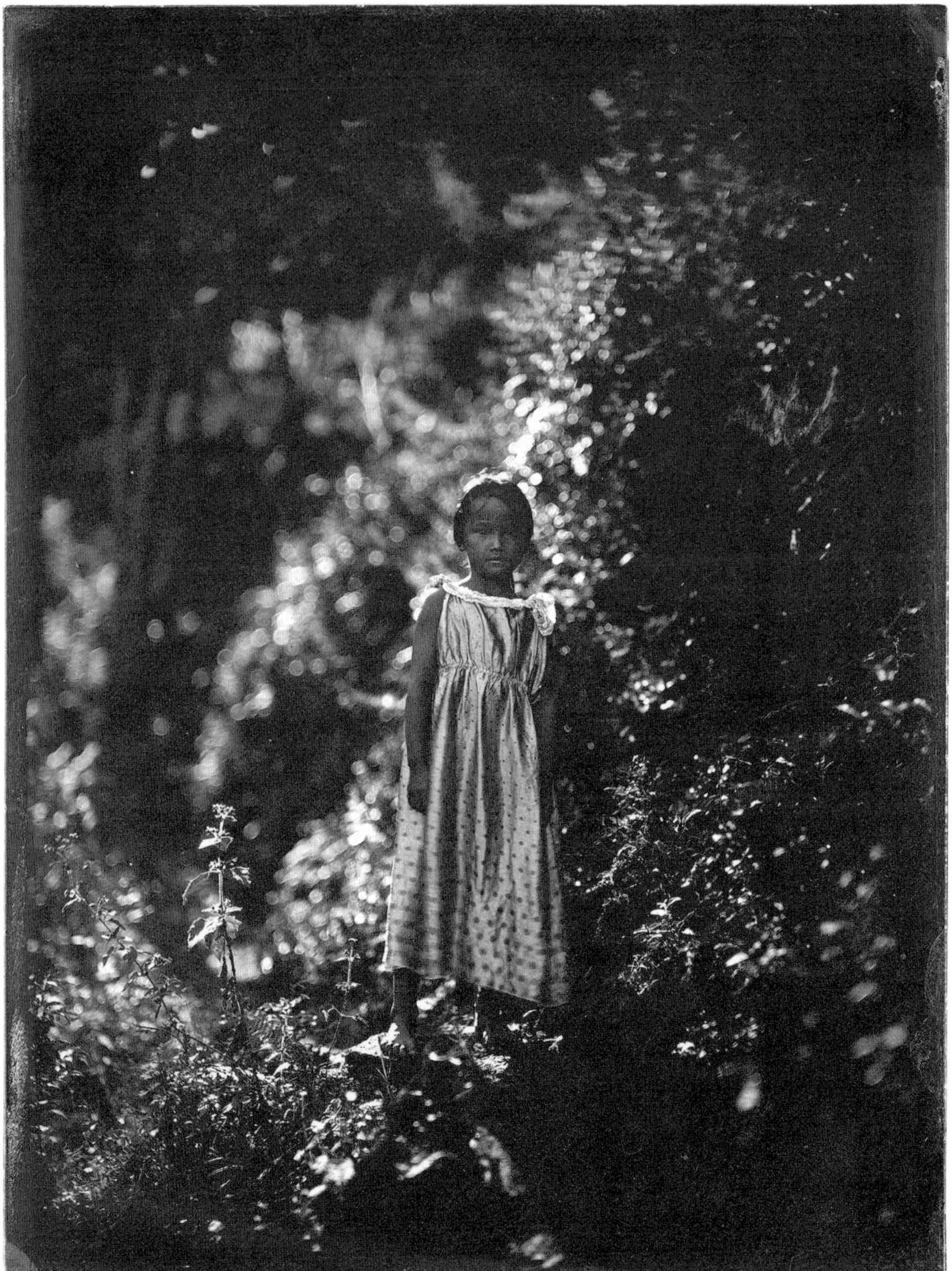

Luo Dan
Simple Song No. 30
La Huana, Chihengdi Village
2010

BARBARA YIEN

Two Poems

THE WHITE TERROR

Taiwan, 1947–1987

The ink on the paper kept disappearing.
Even the permanent. Even the sickle-celled.

The afterlife of tongues
sliced from the mouths of the mouse-trapped
served up for their descendants,
plated—

Then a waiter whisked away the plates.

Then the characters on the menu
(the one hidden from Westerners)
re-assembled, were rendered
un-translatable.

Fastidiously scrubbed.

Efficient as the cleaner in a gangster
film who wipes cerebrum
from linoleum, then vanishes.

SMALL POTATO IN THE MOONLIGHT

Gu Cheng's* drawings turned macabre.
His windows slammed shut.
His small potato in the moonlight
came to resemble the sad-
sack shape of a fallen man.
A dog paused to sniff him, then was gone.

* *A Misty poet of the early 1980s, Gu Cheng went into exile; in 1993, suffering from depression, he committed suicide.*

FIONA SZE-LORRAIN

Five Poems

I WAIT FOR THE RUINED ELEGANCE

Plum blossoms comb the southern mountain. Maybe

winter,
maybe spring. What is the difference

between two seasons? If

only swallows mend the wind, the immaculate river—
from tree to tree, grievance

                                        by grievance. I watch
the sun turn from a sphere to a palace. Burning,

but not disastrous. Soon, but not

now, my gaze
will break. I want to honor

the invisible. And I'll use the fog to see white peaches.

AM I WHAT THE LAKE GAVE ME

In recurring gestures this round wardrobe of tears deletes its soul. Only strangers require faces. Not everyone desires contradiction. They called my teacher sorceress before she drowned here. The rest, a matter not of reason. This is why our grief tastes like water. The children associate it with punishment. They have forgotten that water is an herb. The sorceress will wake up at no distance. But I tell myself I am safe. Five points and two maps, we are not from here, stopping to read signs from above. What a perfect question, a useless mirror.

NEITHER AN ELEGY NOR A DREAM

My grandfather caught a tiger in a stone, and could carve a stone into a tiger. He wasn't an angry man. He built bridges and cupboards. Leaving behind twelve rabbits and a foundation. The bed he made for me surrendered its shape when my body suspended a mountain in me. Now and then I asked the door if he'd return with clothes he died in. His noble face, too discreet to weep. The shaman believed that I betrayed my clairvoyance. *Quick, swallow all the coins you've stolen.* The dead always punish odd spirits. In my sleep, a vulture was arranging its feathers at my feet. I fidgeted but held intact my laughter. Premonition ended like a fruit fallen. In defeat, in plain colors. My grandfather initiated our pact. No time to fall ill, no time to heal. I wasn't young, but I was forgiven. I took the same road, braved the same sun. I rode on shadows and looked for white. Trying to memorize our last time.

REFUSING LYRICISM

This sadness in me isn't mine. An earthen jar, Emily Dickinson, and a bed. The wait most of all. It became the space, a cell that ran on dark feet in my mind. If the wait is sinister, change yourself to hours. To something fickle that serves as flesh and spirit. I chanted and drew a blue fox on each wall. So badly, so well. My American friends write poems on war and imprisonment. Both political and spiritual. Is their imprisonment a concept a subject an inspiration. I've lived through both, childless and don't need lies.

TROUVILLE, 2011

By the sea the past comes tiding from toes to fingers. Rising or falling, we hear the break of us. We come to heal because a child left us. Can't you see the horizon coming in many lines. The sun arrives on time and leaves on the mark. Let's pray for a harbor that has no owner. With sand and oyster shells I stage an opera. In many castles and mansions devoid of persona. I stick half-cigarettes in the wet sand, pretending they play miniature soldiers who prey on absence and white fear. They're trying to breathe, but the struggle is permanent. I'll control the pain, make the scream formless. With confused trees and gods, the world is a budget theater. For a long time we have not been alone. Room after room, people walk in and out. Most of them need something from us. Perhaps I'll eat *mussels marinières* tonight. With or without fries. It is too early to predict movement. Do you really know how to feel empty. Nine times out of ten, it is an accident. One sand castle falls, then more. And all.

About the Contributors

Amang 阿芒 (1964–) was born and raised in Hualien County, on the east coast of Taiwan. She is the author of two volumes of verse, *On/Off: Selected Poems of Amang, 1995–2002* (2003), and *No Daddy* (2008). Her poetry has been published in several Taiwanese journals, including *Poetry Now* and *Off the Roll: Poetry+*. She works as an English teacher in Taipei and is a student of video documentation.

Bai Hua 柏桦 (1956–) was born in Chongqing in Southwest China. He studied English literature at Guangzhou Foreign Language Institute before graduating with a master's degree in Western literary history from Sichuan University. He is considered the central literary figure of the post-Obscure (or post-Misty) poetry movement of the 1980s. His first collection of poems, *Expression* (1988), received immediate critical acclaim. He is admired today by a large audience in China. He received the 2001 Anne Kao Poetry Prize and in 2007 the prestigious Rougang Poetry Award. He currently lives in Chengdu, Sichuan, where he teaches at Southwest Jiaotong University.

Bei Dao 北岛 (1949–) is the pen name of Zhao Zhenkai, born in Beijing. In 1976, his poetry gained recognition among activists in the PRC democracy movement, and in 1978 he cofounded with Mang Ke the literary magazine *Jintian* (Today). In 1980, the magazine was banned by the Chinese government. In the early 1980s, Bei Dao worked for the Foreign Languages Press in Beijing and became a target of the government's Anti-Spiritual Pollution Campaign. His poetry began to be published outside the PRC in 1983, and he traveled to Europe and the United States. His 1986 collection, *Bei Dao shi xuan*, published in English as *The August Sleepwalker*, was also banned by authorities. During the June 1989 suppression of pro-democracy demonstrations in Tian'anmen Square, he was traveling in Germany, but was accused by the government of helping to incite the events in the square. He chose exile, along with his friends Duo Duo, Yang Lian, and Gu Cheng, who were also abroad then. With the help of former contributors to *Jintian*, he reestablished the journal as a forum for Chinese writers abroad. He is now an American citizen. He teaches at the Chinese University of Hong Kong.

Chen Yuhong 陳育虹 (1952–) was born in Kaohsiung, Taiwan. She lived for many years in Vancouver before returning to Taipei. Her first poetry collection, *About Poetry*, was published in 1996. Her work includes *In Fact, Sea* (1999), *River Streams Deep into Your Veins* (2002), *Annotations* (2004), and *Between* (2011). She is the

Chinese translator of *Rapture*, by British poet laureate Carol Ann Duffy, and *La Citadelle des neiges*, a book of spirituality and fables by Matthieu Ricard, a French Tibetan Buddhist monk.

Duo Yu 朵渔 (1973–) was born in Shandong Province and is one of the founding members of the Lower Body Movement, based in Beijing during the early 2000s. He received the 2007 Rougang Poetry Award and the 2010 Chinese Literature Media Award, and is the author of two collections of poetry, *Chasing Butterflies* (2009) and *Writing Little Poems Causes Worries* (2010). His several books of prose include *Meanings Have Bored Us* (2003) and *Ten Faces* (2009). He lives in Tianjin.

Hai Zi 海子 (1964–1989) was born and raised in a farming village in Anhui Province. When he was fifteen, he passed the entrance exam for the prestigious Beijing University, and at twenty he started teaching philosophy and art theory at China University of Political Science and Law. Between 1984 and 1989, he wrote over two hundred poems and several epics. He committed suicide in March 1989 by lying down in front of an oncoming train at Beijing Shanhaiguan. Published posthumously in China, his books include *Earth* (1990), *Works of Hai Zi and Luo Yihe* (1991), *Poems of Hai Zi* (1995), *The Complete Works of Hai Zi* (1997), *Hai Zi* (2006), *Selected Works of Hai Zi* (2006), and *Poetry of Hai Zi* (2007).

Brian Holton was educated in Chinese studies at the University of Edinburgh and did postgraduate research at Durham University. He was the Leverhulme research associate in the Department of Chinese at the University of Edinburgh, working on the Jin Shengtan Project from 1985 to 1988, and later taught Chinese at the University of Edinburgh. He has held many university posts in the PRC, the United Kingdom, and elsewhere. Among his current projects is the translation of T'ang poet Du Fu into Scottish.

Lan Lan 蓝蓝 (1967–) is the pen name of Hu Lanlan, born in Yantai, Shandong Province. At fourteen, she published her first sequence of poems, "I Want to Sing." Her books include *Life with a Smile* (1990), *Songs of Romance* (1993), *Inner Life* (1997), *Dream, Dream* (2003), and *From Here, to Here* (2008). In addition to writing poetry, she is also a prolific prose and children's fiction writer. In 2009, she received four national literary awards: the Poetry and People Award, the Yulong Poetry Prize, the Best Ten Poets in China Award, and the Bing Xin Children's Literature New Work Award. She lives in Beijing.

Karen An-hwei Lee (1973–) was born in Massachusetts. She is the author of *Ardor* (2008) and *In Medias Res* (2004), winner of the Kathryn A. Morton Prize and the Norma Farber First Book Award. Her chapbook, *God's One Hundred Promises* (2002), received the Swan Scythe Press Prize. Two new collections of her work are forthcoming from Tupelo Press. She is the chair of the English department at a faith-based university in southern California.

Li Shangyin 李商隱 (813–858) was born in Henan Province. A late-T'ang Dynasty poet, his works are known for their atmosphere and enigmatic depth, making his poems difficult to translate. He held low-level posts as a government official, and although he was appreciated in certain literary circles during his lifetime, his importance was not recognized until the twentieth century.

Ling Yu 零雨 (1952–) was born in the mountains of Taipei County. She received her bachelor's degree in Chinese from National Taiwan University and her master's degree in East Asian languages and literatures from the University of Wisconsin–Madison. Her books of poems include *Series on a City* (1990), *Names Lost on a Map* (1992), *An Acrobat Family* (1996), *Collected Songs of Winter Trees* (1999), *Recountings of the Hometown* (2006), and *I Am Heading for You* (2010). She was the chief editor of *Modern Poetry Quarterly* from 1986 to 1992 and now teaches at National Ilan University, outside of Taipei.

Luo Dan 骆丹 (1968–) was born in Chongqing and graduated from the Sichuan Fine Art Academy in 1992. A portrait and documentary photographer, he has won awards and recognition for his works *On the Road—Highway 318* (2006) and *North, South* (2008). For *North, South*, he received the Gold Award for Outstanding Artist at the 2008 Lianzhou International Photography Festival. He has also received the Hou Dengke documentary photography prize and in 2011 was voted best new photographer at the Dali International Photography Festival. He lives and works in Chengdu.

Dechen Pemba was born in the United Kingdom, was educated in London, and has lived in Berlin and Beijing. She publishes the blog *High Peaks Pure Earth* (highpeakspureearth.com), which features the translated writings of Tibetans living in Tibet and China. After teaching English in Beijing for two years, she was detained and expelled from the PRC in 2008. She was accused of being a member of the radical Tibetan Youth Congress and being involved in "activities against Chinese laws." Pemba has denied the charges and continues to blog from London.

Denis Mair has worked as a translator in Beijing and studied in a Daoist-Confucian temple in Taiwan. His translations include the memoirs of Buddhist monk Shih Chen-hua, an autobiography of philosopher Feng Youlan, and fiction by Wang Meng, China's former Minister of Culture. Mair published a collection of his own poetry, *Man Cut in Wood,* in 2003.

Thomas Moran is the John D. Berninghausen professor of Chinese at Middlebury College, where he teaches Chinese language, literature, and film. He is the editor of *The Dictionary of Literary Biography: Chinese Fiction Writers, 1900–1949* (2007), and is coediting a second volume in the series. He lives in Ripton, Vermont.

Pang Pei 庞培 (1962–) was born in Suying, Jiangsu Province. After he completed junior high school, his family's economic circumstances compelled him to leave school. He first worked in shipyards and later in textile factories. In 1985, he published his first novel, and in 1988, his poems began to appear in newspapers and magazines. Affectionately known among his peers as the "Poet of the Rain," he is a recipient of the 1995 Liu Li'an Poetry Prize and the 1997 Rougang Poetry Award. He is the author of several collections of poetry and prose, including *Whisper* (1998), *Book of Melancholy* (2000), *Three-Quarter Rain* (2009), and *Various Verses* (2011).

Chloe Garcia Roberts is a poet and translator living in the Boston area. Her work has appeared, or is forthcoming, in *Poetry International*, *Cerise Press*, and *Zoland Poetry*. She is an editor at *Zoland Poetry* and the associate curator of the Woodberry Poetry Room at Harvard, where she helped establish the Omniglot Translation Seminar series.

Sun Lei 孙磊 (1971–) was born in Jinan, Shandong Province, and became a key figure of the post-1970s Chinese poets. His 2005 collection, *Perform*, was one of the ten bestselling poetry titles of the year. Recipient of the 2000 Rougang Poetry Award, he is the founding editor of the literary journal *Who*. Also an accomplished painter and installation artist, he teaches at Central Academy of Fine Arts and Shandong University of Arts. He lives in Beijing and Jinan with his wife, poet Yu Xiang, and their son.

Arthur Sze (1950–) was born in New York City and educated at the University of California–Berkeley. His books of poetry include *River River* (1987), *Archipelago* (1995), *The Redshifting Web* (1998), *Quipu* (2005), and *The Gingko Light* (2009). His books as a translator of Chinese poetry include *The Willow Wind* (1972), *Two Ravens* (1976), and *The Silk Dragon* (2001). In 2010, he edited the collection *Chinese Writers on Writing*. Sze's honors include a Lannan Literary Award, an American Book Award, the Lila Wallace–Reader's Digest Writer's Award, and a Western States Book Award for Translation. He has received grants and fellowships from the Guggenheim Foundation, the National Endowment for the Arts, and the Witter Bynner Foundation for Poetry. He lives in Santa Fe, New Mexico.

Fiona Sze-Lorrain (1980–) was born in Singapore and educated at Columbia University, New York University, and Paris IV–Sorbonne, where she received a doctorate in French. She writes and translates in English, French, and Chinese. Her first collection of poetry, *Water the Moon*, was published in 2010. She is an editor at *Cerise Press* and Vif Éditions. Also a *zheng* concertist, she lives in Paris, France.

Wei An 苇岸 (1960–1999) was the pen name of Ma Jianguo. He grew up on the outskirts of Beijing and studied philosophy at People's University. While in college he was influenced by the Misty poets and their work, befriended the poet Gu Cheng, and began publishing poetry. In 1986, the poet Hai Zi introduced Wei An to Thoreau's *Walden*; inspired by the book, Wei An turned from poetry to prose in the style of Thoreau's observations. Wei An's name is unfamiliar to most Chinese readers, but he is well remembered by poets, writers, and critics. Sections of his *Things on Earth* were first published in 1991.

Woeser 唯色 (1966–) was born in Lhasa and is one-quarter Han Chinese and three-quarters Tibetan. Exiled from Tibet, she now lives in Beijing. She was awarded the Norwegian Authors Union's Freedom of Expression Prize, the freedom of speech medal from the Association of Tibetan Journalists, and the International Women's Media Foundation's Courage in Journalism Award. Most recently, she was selected for the Prince Claus Award by the Dutch for her courage in reporting about Tibet while living in the PRC, but the Chinese government prevented her from receiving the award by placing her under house arrest.

Yang Changhong 杨长虹 (1979–) was born in Anshun, Guizhou Province. He has participated in various international photography exhibitions in Pingyao, Lianzhou, New York, and Paris. He is a photojournalist at the *Nanfang Metropolis* news organization, in Guangdong Province.

Yang Lian 杨炼 (1955–) was born in Switzerland and grew up in Beijing. In the 1970s, he began writing when he was sent to the countryside for "re-education" during the Cultural Revolution. On his return to Beijing, he became one of the founders of the Misty school. In 1988, he was invited to visit Australia and New Zealand; in June 1989, the Tian'anmen Square demonstrations took place, and he became a poet-in-exile. He has continued to write and speak out on world literature, politics, and culture and has published eleven collections of poetry, two of prose, and one of essays. Along with Scottish poet W. N. Herbert and translator Brian Holton, Yang Lian is the coeditor of *Jade Ladder*, a 2011 anthology of contemporary Chinese poetry translated into English. His latest work is *The Narrative Poem*, a book-length poem based on his experiences. The first edition of the book was confiscated and destroyed by Chinese officials because of its inclusion of "Reality Elegy," a poem with references to the Tian'anmen Square events. Since 2005, he has been the artistic director of Unique Mother Tongue, an international seminar series based in London.

Yang Zi 杨子 (1963–) was born in Anhui Province and is the author of a dozen books, including *Border Fast Train* (1994), *Gray Eyes* (2000), and *Rouge* (2007). After completing his university studies in Chinese literature, he lived in Xinjiang Uygur Autonomous Region for nine years and cofounded the literary journal *Big Bird*. In 1990, he was appointed vice alderman of Tahaqi Village. Since 1993, he has lived in Guangzhou, and he is now the associate chief editor of the *Nanfang People Weekly*. Also known as a poetry translator, he has introduced the writings of Osip Mandelstam, Paul Celan, Fernando Pessoa, Theodore Roethke, Gary Snyder, Charles Simic, and other Western poets to Chinese readers.

Michelle Yeh was born and raised in Taiwan. She received her doctorate in comparative literature from the University of Southern California and has been teaching at the University of California–Davis since 1988. A scholar and translator, she has published more than a dozen books, including *Modern Chinese Poetry: Theory and Practice Since 1917, Anthology of Modern Chinese Poetry* (edited and translated into English, 1994), *No Trace of the Gardener: Poems of Yang Mu* (cotranslated into English, 1998), *Essays on Modern Chinese Poetry* (in Chinese, 1998), *From the Margin: An Alternative Tradition of Modern Chinese Poetry* (in Chinese, 2000), *Frontier Taiwan: An Anthology of Modern Chinese Poetry* (coedited and cotranslated; English and Chinese editions, 2001), and *Iconography of the Sea: Poems of Derek Walcott* (translated into Chinese, 2001).

Yi Lu 伊路 (1956–) is the author of five books of poetry, including *See* (2004) and *Using Two Seas* (2009). Her latest volume, *Forever Lingering*, was published in 2011. Her honors include the Hundred Flowers Award for Literature and the Distinguished Literary Prize from Fujian Province. She is a stage designer at the People's Art Theatre in Fujian and lives in Fuzhou.

Barbara Yien (1975–) has been published widely in American journals. She now lives in Berkeley, California, working as a textbook editor.

Yinni 隱匿 (1969–) is the pen name of a Taiwanese poet who, with her husband, runs Youhe Books, an independent bookstore in Danshuei District, New Taipei City. Her third and most recent book of poetry is *How Can It Be* (2011).

Yu Xiang 宇向 (1970–) has published a chapbook, *Sorceress* (2002); a volume of poetry, *Exhale* (2006); and a forthcoming collection, *I Can Almost See the Clouds of Dust*. She has received the 2002 Rougang Poetry Award and the 2006 Yulong Poetry Prize. She lives in Jinan, Shandong Province.

Zeng Han 曾翰 (1974–) was born in Guangdong. He received a bachelor's degree in international journalism and communication from Jinan University in Guangzhou in 1997. In 2009, he completed a residency program at the School of Visual Arts in New York. His photography has appeared in many exhibitions in the PRC, Australia, the U.S., and Europe. He recently had a solo exhibition in New York, *Soul Stealer + Cool Shanshui*, and was part of a group exhibition in Beijing, *The Three Shadows Photo Award 2010 Exhibition*.

Zhang Zao 张枣 (1962–2010) was a key figure of the "third generation" of Chinese contemporary poets and rose to national fame as one of the "Five Sichuan Masters." He was also a literary critic, translator, and scholar of German literature and philosophy. In 1986, he moved to Germany, where he married, and earned a doctorate in literature from Tübingen University. For several years, he served as poetry editor of *Jintian*. He returned briefly to China in 2005 to teach world literature at various universities. At the age of forty-eight, he died in Tübingen. Fewer than ninety of his poems survive.

About the Photographs by Luo Dan

To photograph the images in his *Simple Song* project, Luo Dan lived in close contact with people of the Lisu ethnic minority, in the remote, rural mountains of Yunnan's Nujiang Lisu Autonomous Prefecture. Lisu villages are on the cultural, linguistic, and geographic periphery of modern China and are often isolated from Han settlements. As a result of proselytizing by Western missionaries in the late-nineteenth and early-twentieth centuries, many Lisu people are Christians.

Luo Dan was drawn to the Lisu people because he saw in their rustic way of life values of purity and authenticity that are missing in modern, industrial society. Beginning in 2010, Luo patiently stayed in remote villages for up to six months. To capture the timeless qualities that he admired in Lisu people, he decided to photograph them using the collodion wet plate process, invented in the 1850s and later replaced by simpler, less costly techniques. Wet plate collodion images can produce exquisite detail, but the process requires a light-sensitive emulsion to be prepared on a glass plate using hazardous chemicals, such as acetic acid and ferrous sulfate. Once the emulsion is ready, the plate must be exposed while still wet, then developed before it dries. The light sensitivity of collodion plates is quite low, so exposure can take a minute or more, during which time the subject must remain perfectly still.

Some of the remarkable images by Luo Dan shown in *Sky Lanterns* are of Lisu people wearing their Sunday best, having come from church services. Luo Dan says he chose the collodion wet plate process "to preserve the magical spiritual lights" in these places.

Acknowledgments

Bai Hua, "Afternoon," "To Osip Mandelstam," "Spring Begins," and "The Tibetan," translated by Fiona Sze-Lorrain, from *Wind Says* (Zephyr Press, forthcoming).

Hai Zi, "The Source and the Bird," translated by Fiona Sze-Lorrain, from *Wheat Has Ripened* (Tupelo Press, forthcoming).

Lan Lan, "Lost," "Disappear," "Ruins of the Great River Village," and "Unfinished Voyage," translated by Fiona Sze-Lorrain, from *Canyon in the Body* (Zephyr Press, forthcoming).

Wei An, from "Life on Earth," translated by Thomas Moran, from *Things on Earth* (1991).

Yang Lian, "Baby Girl," translated by Brian Holton, appeared in *Chutzpah 3* (August 2011) in a slightly different version.

Yi Lu, "An Old Tree," translated by Fiona Sze-Lorrain, first appeared in *Poetry Salzburg Review* (2011).

Yu Xiang, "It Goes Without Saying," "A Painting Life," "Like Humans," "Sorceress," "Window," "Fantasia of a Housefly," and "Crossing Night," translated by Fiona Sze-Lorrain, from *I Can Almost See the Clouds of Dust* (Zephyr Press, forthcoming).

Zhang Zao, "Elegy," "Letters in Four Seasons," and "World," translated by Fiona Sze-Lorrain, from *Mirror* (Zephyr Press, forthcoming).

DISCOVER CHINA

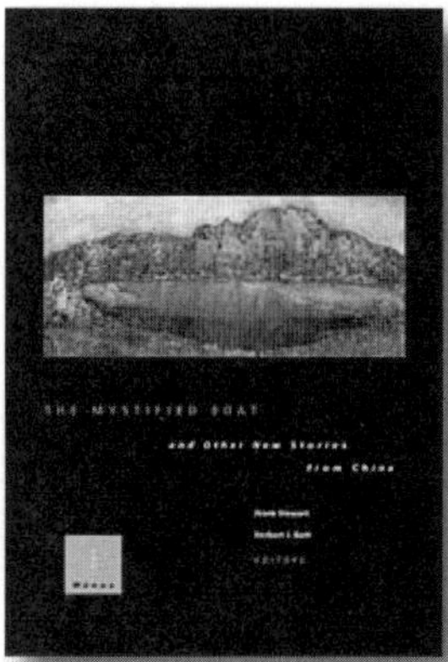

THE MYSTIFIED BOAT
POSTMODERN STORIES FROM CHINA

Guest-edited by Herbert J. Batt

Through radical experiments with fiction, China's most innovative and best-known postmodernists question the meaning of "story" and the many conventions that drive our assumptions about narrators and narration. Featuring Ma Yuan, Ma Jian, Ge Fei, Hong Ying, Su Tong, Lin Bai, Yan Li, Can Xue, Wang Anyi, and Yu Hua.

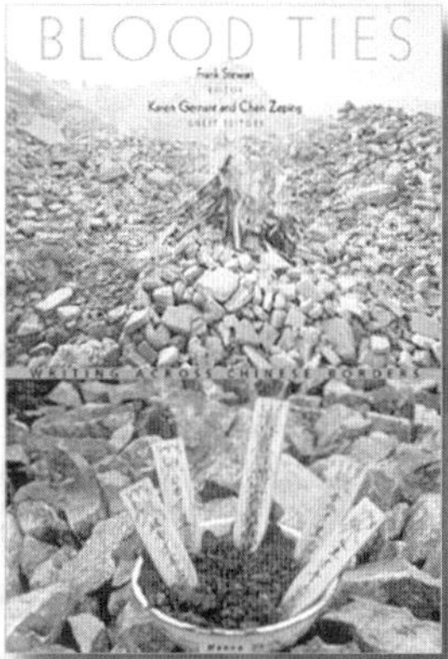

BLOOD TIES
WRITING ACROSS CHINESE BORDERS

Guest-edited by Karen Gernant and Chen Zeping

In fiction, poetry, nonfiction, and artwork, this collection explores the complexities of Chinese identity created by migration, displacement, ethnic mixing, and separation from home. Authors include Alai, Zhang Kangkang, Zhu Wenying, Zhang Er, Wang Ping, Arthur Sze, Yan Li, Catherine Lim, Colin Cheong, Rex Shelley, and Yi writer Aku Wuwu.

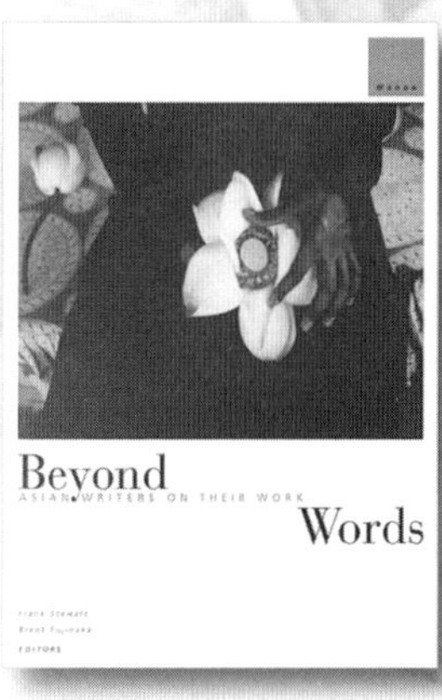

BEYOND WORDS
ASIAN WRITERS ON THEIR WORK

Guest-edited by Brent Fujinaka

More than two dozen authors from China, Tibet, Japan, Korea, the Philippines, Indonesia, Viet Nam, Cambodia, and Malaysia discuss the art of writing. Their essays, interviews, stories, and poems present a full range of perspectives shaped by nationality, language, age, gender, and aesthetics.

available online at

http://muse.jhu.edu • http://www.jstor.org